LIVING IN FRANCE MADE SIMPLE

By

Tanja Bulatovic

Copyright 2012 Tanja Bulatovic

Disclaimer: I have taken every effort to provide accurate information in this guide. As far as I am aware the information I have included is correct as of writing; however, the reader takes full responsibility for verifying all information. The content presented here is provided "AS IS" without warranty of any kind. I don't profess to provide all the answers here. There is no such thing as a definitive way of doing things; a one-size-fits-all method for every individual. This guide is a mix of my personal experience, opinion and practical information. I decline all responsibility regarding the use of information in this guide. The reader takes full responsibility for any damages, harm, or fees incurred from using the information presented in this guide. Any links mentioned within this book are for educational and informational purposes only. They are not affiliate links. I do not stand to profit financially from any of the links listed in this guide.

For Fabrice

"C'est a partir de toi que j'ai dit oui au monde."

Paul Eluard

Contents

Introduction…6

Chapter 1, Making it Happen…8

Peasant Girl Philosophy…8

Why France…11

Visas, Cartes De Sejours/ Residency and Work Permits…17

Retiring in France…23

How to work in France…23

Embassies and Consulates…24

Marrying a French citizen…25

How to become a French citizen…26

How to Integrate (even if you don't feel like it)…27

Chapter 2, Practicalities…29

The Cost of Living…29

Learning the Language…34

Health Care in France…40

Educating your Child in France…43

Driving in France…47

Working in France…50

Art for Art's sake…55

Opening a Bank Account in France…59

French Taxes…61

Moving your Pet to France…63

France - Warts and all…63

Checklist for Documents Needed…67

More Resources…68

Chapter 3, Food, Love and Wine…70

Food Laws and Rituals…71

Surviving France as a Vegetarian…75

Pass the Real Fromage…78

Wine…79

Food and Politics…82

Expat Isolation…84

Dating in France (a tale of everyday seduction)…87

Links for Paris lovers…93

Chapter 4, Your Own Home in France…95

Your Real Estate Dream Come True…96

Freedom for less than €50 000…97

Step-by-Step Guide to Buying Property in France…98

France Regions and Real Estate Prices Overview (including links to latest listings)…102

List of Real Estate Agents…111

Secret Real-Estate Hot Spots…115

Finding Short and Long-Term Rentals…116

Real Estate Extra…118

Epilogue…119

About the Author…120

Other books by Tanja Bulatovic…120

Contact Details…120

Introduction

A few years ago I wrote an article for EscapeArtist entitled 'Living in Marseille'. In a nutshell, the plot went something like this:

'Heartbroken and hopeless 40-year old girl/ woman meets and falls in love with a Frenchman who then entices her to follow him (from Australia) to France. They get married. New chapter. New life.'

It was the first article I'd ever written, and consequently the first article I'd ever had published. Much to my surprise, the warm feedback I received (thank you warm feedback people!) was so overwhelming it inspired me to write something more substantial.

Among other frivolous occupations, I'm a classically trained actor and a self-taught writer. An ordinary person who put her heart on the table with nothing to lose - wanting to convince people that if she could move to a new country and start a new life, so could they.

Writing that first article felt like a culmination of everything that had happened to me up until that point. Like a *denouemont* or end of a big chapter and at the same time a door to a new beginning.

And though I'm not yet sure where this new beginning will lead, for now I'm happy to be walking you through my experience. Grateful for the opportunity to share my story in the hope of inspiring and contributing to the 'collective unconscious' that seems to be floating around right now.

You know what I mean, right?

It's like a universal heartbeat...telling us that some kind of change is in the air.

Can you feel it? If you can't, you need to listen to your deepest self.

The future has never felt more murky, unclear and unsafe. Maybe in the past but certainly not in my lifetime. Until now. You see now, there's something else at stake. We are no longer simply fantasizing about moving to the other side of the planet on a whim. This is about something else entirely. It's about survival.

Can we honestly afford to wait for more global shocks or a personal crisis to change our lives in a dramatic way? We need to look at our core values. We need to make a new life for our families and ourselves. And we need to do it NOW. The time is NOW, not somewhere in the future.

As far as the future is concerned, what can we be certain of?

Only this: **Along with disaster, destruction and catastrophe comes opportunity to change things for the better. Not change things back to how they where before, but a new kind of better.**

Now, more than ever, I ache for a small patch of land, some simple living, nature and a life that revolves around a vegetable garden. It seems I'm not the only one. Yet for many people living elsewhere in the world (Australia, US, UK to name a few), that dream has become unrealistic. Out of reach.

If nothing else, I'm here to tell you the dream is still achievable in France.

So these here are the fragments of a long story. A story of how I came to be free. And even though this is my story it could just as easily be yours. But in these pages rests more than simply my story; you will find a compilation and guide consisting of information that's taken me years to accumulate and mostly the hard way.

That being said, if you are longing for a new kind of freedom, take my hand. As some wise person once said, there's no time like the present. And there's no country in the world that comes closer to understanding the beauty of the present moment.

No country like France.

Chapter 1
Making it Happen

"One day your life will flash before your eyes. Make sure it's worth watching."
(Unknown)

Peasant Girl Philosophy

Once upon a time, in Australia, I stopped at a flower booth to buy some blossoms for a friend. There was an old man inside the booth by the name of 'Basil'. As he carefully wrapped my roses, we started chatting.

"And what do you do for a living young lady?"

"Oh, I don't know" I said, "I guess I've done a lot of different stuff, but mostly I like to move around."

"Yes", he replied as he steadily tied the bow…

"We travel the world looking for who we are but we come home to find out."

I've never forgotten that conversation. Not only did Basil's comment resonate; it left me with a giant question.

Where the hell is home?

Some people find it easy to answer that question, but for others like me, it's been a life-long quest. Basil was obviously talking about a sense of inner peace one reaches when one is content. Of the ultimate home being ones interior landscape. And he's right, of course, but the exterior is just as important, don't you think?

If the exterior isn't supporting you, how can you possible feel ready to excavate the interior? You probably know what I mean if you've ever asked yourself the "Who ordered *this* life?" question. Surely you have, otherwise you wouldn't be reading up on living in France. But your motivation probably stems from a number of factors…

- Change is good
- You're not happy
- Deep down you know you're only sticking around out of habit; it's what you know
- You're struggling financially, locked into wage-slavery and looking for a way out
- You know that a life that's 'good enough' isn't necessarily good enough for you
- Because you know that the right country, the right location will buy you some time
- Because not living the life you want to live is stressful
- Because you know that happiness comes through experiences, not things
- Because you want your whole life to resemble a work of art
- Because you know that simplifying your life (more on that later) gives you the opportunity to

live your life, gives you your life back
- Because you've got big concerns about your future in today's world
- Because you have a crush on all things French
- Because you want adventure
- Because you want to buy a home in France
- You just got a divorce
- You're in the throws of a mid-life crisis
- Because you've got a shitty view

Over the years, I have felt most of the above without being able to articulate exactly what I was feeling. So if this is an 'Aha' moment for you, then we're on the same page. Good news is that dreaming is free. And so are nice views; but in order to see clearly, you need to position yourself right. How? By getting out of your own way. And when you do, you will see that 'living the dream' in France (or anywhere else for that matter) really is well and truly within your reach.

While searching for answers, truth, nirvana, call it what you will, I've read hundreds of books, bought out of sheer desperation and frustration because they 'made a promise' of a better life (plus they sounded super exciting in the sales pitch). Needless to say I signed up for many a dream, and devoured every piece of information. And sure enough, the books more or less fulfilled what they set out to, but in the end, I always felt a little disappointed.

Why? I guess I'd expected something different. Something more than practical facts - a free plane ticket to the Seychelles stashed inside the book probably wouldn't have gone astray (pre eBooks, this could have been possible).

You see I didn't want just the facts. I wanted to read that someone like me was already doing it. But most of all, I wanted to be inspired, and to know the dream was actually possible. Having said that, I also wanted the writer to take off the mask and give me something more than the stereotypical images. Not an airbrushed version. The real thing. Warts and all.

By the time I finished reading the books, I usually felt so overwhelmed by the big picture and all that was required to immigrate to Timbuktu, re-invent myself and/ or live a transnational life, I lost my nerve to follow through.

Looking back, I guess when it came down to it, I had 'decided' that I couldn't do it. Seemingly, there was always some minor detail sabotaging my efforts, which at the time felt too hopeless to even contemplate:

Wrong passport, no money, no real career, debts = not a chance in hell.

Back then I had no idea how wrong I was.

My driving purpose in building this guide was to create something inspirational, fun and useful. A mix of practical information and every-day observations topped with some heart, soul and a little dream dust to ignite your imagination. I know. I know. No easy task, but I promise I did my best.

My deepest wish, however, is this: That when you read these words, you'll be nourished and inspired to act, or to at least think about things in a different way. The reason 99.9 percent of people don't make the leap is fear. But you already know that. I know a bit about that too.

Don't worry, I'm not about to stand on the soapbox and tell you to 'face your fears'. It's a term too well trodden and nearly all self-growth-talk makes me nauseous.

But I will say this: Most of us were taught to make safe choices instead of reaching for rich life experiences. It's only a matter of re-adjusting and getting better at being courageous. It's also about grabbing life by the balls.

When nothing else works, occasionally I remind myself of this: This play called 'life', it's not a rehearsal before you get to perform in the real thing. This is it. Unfortunately most of us are living the rehearsal and we're in denial. And for many, the 'sleepwalk-through', as it stands, is a bloody mess.

Why?

- The stage and costumes aren't ready
- The lighting guy hasn't arrived yet
- We've forgotten our lines (which weren't all that interesting anyway)
- Now if we could only find the director to tell us what to do

> "We are always getting ready to live but never living."
>
> (Ralph Waldo Emerson)

Ralph knew it. And so do you, which is why you're here. Therefore, if your life at the moment looks anything like mine used to…

Zero money, no career, wrong passport, debts and broken heart infested by cockroaches, you've come to the right place.

I'm living proof that things *can* change for the better. That, pending on a few simple choices, decisions and changes, an ordinary person can live an extraordinary life in the country of their dreams.

Don't listen to the killjoys. If you really want to live in France it can be done. Listening to other people inevitably means nothing will ever happen. Unquestionably, it's a lot easier to do nothing. To stay at home, glued to the television for fear of another natural or man-made disaster. But if the world truly is coming to an end, I for one don't want to watch it in slow motion on TV. I'm guessing neither do you.

But before we get into the thick of things I'd like to say 'thank you'. Thanks for reading. For enabling me to paint you my version of the picture. I don't profess to be the best painter, though my lack of skill is compensated by my enthusiasm for setting you free.

You, in fact, are nothing *but* freedom. And sure, France is only but one spot in which to thrive, but I'm here to tell you; it's a pretty damn good one.

> "Man is free at the moment he wishes to be."
>
> (Voltaire)

Why France?

To this day, I'm not sure whether it was destiny or a sort of subconscious longing that brought me to France. But for as long as I can remember, I've had a silly fascination for all things French.

When I was 16 years old, a black and white photographic print in a shop window stopped me in my tracks. It was, I thought at the time, the most romantic image I'd ever seen.

A couple kissing in the streets of Paris in the 1950s. The print, by French photographer Robert Doisneau entitled "Kiss, by the Hotel de Ville", was and probably still is one of his best-known works. So as soon as I saved up the rather hefty $150, I bought it and stuck it on my bedroom wall.

You know it, right? Just in case you have no idea what I'm talking about (it happens), google 'Robert Doisneau - Kiss by the Hotel de Ville', and you'll see what I mean.

In addition to the black and white print, I became infatuated with French cinema, French actors and actresses, French music, food, and fashion. I listened endlessly, as if possessed, to Edith Piaf, Yves Montand, Jaques Brel and Charles Aznavour. Although I didn't have a clue about what they were singing, I suppose the music must have fulfilled something, some longing in me.

What happened after that?

Oh yeah, that's right…when I grew up, destiny placed an unsuspecting Frenchman in my path. His name was Fabrice, and just as soon as he stepped out of the black and white print, I married him. Surprised???

And here we are.

Admittedly, since moving to France, life hasn't all been chocolates and roses. I've had my fair share of hairy moments and reservations about the place. And when I think about it, the endless red tape, bureaucracy, backwardness, and lack of customer-service are enough to send most people running in the opposite direction.

But the key word here is 'think', which is something I don't do anymore. If you can learn to switch off the thinking part, then that my friends, pretty much takes care of any worries, angst or stress one might be having about the 'system' around these parts.

We need to take the good with the bad. Right?

Here then, is some of the good: Even though the entire world seems to be falling apart, France is still (as of writing) doing pretty well. There are no tsunamis, major earthquakes and/ or governments slaughtering its own people. Relatively speaking, France continues to thrive economically while other European countries have fallen through the cracks.

Why?

Because *La France* is largely self-sufficient - a leading agricultural producer in Western Europe and a major exporter of wheat and dairy products.

As a result, living here is still affordable. Cheap as chips in fact, when compared to countries like Australia or the UK. Real estate prices in particular. Evidently for many of us, most our time, energy and money are tied up in acquiring an oversized and overpriced roof over our heads, which we then maintain and pay off until we die. Insanity? Right on! So why do we do it?

Because a surprising number of us are brainwashed into thinking that trading out lives for an oversized and overpriced roof is 'normal'. What some call normal I call pervasive wage-slavery, but here's where I give you my best French shrug and move on…

Case in point: As much as I adore Australia (my home for almost 30 years), living there is no longer affordable for the average person. Not only have real estate prices gone through the roof, there's a shortage in rental accommodation - with people having to cue for hours in order to 'bid' - auction style - for the most ordinary rental properties. Needless to say, the highest bid wins.

It's not just real estate prices. The general cost of living is sky high. My mother, who is retired and lives by herself, says she's lucky to spend less than $200 per week on food. She's no fancy eater. Mainly fruits, grains, veggies with the occasional morsel of meat. If she didn't own her tiny apartment, I'd hate to think how on earth she would manage. At the time of writing, a standard one-bedroom, 40m2 apartment in the city of Melbourne rents at around $350 per week, plus bills. Fine. Though one needs to consider that the average Australian pension for a single person is something like $667 per fortnight!

Is it any wonder then, that so many baby boomers are becoming expats and bailing out of the 'good retirees' game altogether? And why shouldn't they, when their hard-earned retirement fund or pension stretches much further on foreign soil?

If you are retired and you haven't planned your exit strategy yet, you have options:

For instance, you could…

- Move to a cheaper part of the world (i.e. France)
- Be a perpetual traveler without ever settling anywhere
- Buy a sailing boat
- Live on a houseboat and cruise the canals (in France or elsewhere)
- Chill out in a cabin in the woods and go fishing
- Cruise around in a camping car or VW Kombi

Anything is possible. And it's never too late.

As I said before, the number one reason people stay put is that funny old bugger called fear. How do I know this? Because I keep getting the same questions from readers asking:

Is it safe to live in Marseille?

What about the crime?

The bad reputation?

The terrorist attacks?

The drugs?

The racism?

And sure, I tell them… if you look for it, you'll find bad stuff here like anywhere else. I don't look for it. And I don't hang out in dives and bars with seedy criminals and street gangs (at least not anymore). If you're not into hanging out in unwholesome places and mixing it up with the local mafia, chances are you'll be ok wherever you decide to go. Terrorist attacks? Well, they've become a part of life pretty much all over the planet, haven't they.

On that account, can you honestly say you feel 100 percent safe where you live right now?

This part of the world has its share of problems, that's for sure, but in general it is civilized, tolerant, and social, which is why (as of writing), France still in the list of top 25 best countries to live in the world, for the 7th year in a row, followed by Australia and Switzerland in third place.

And no…it's not all about the cheese, baguette, frog's legs, silly hats, curly moustaches, nuclear bomb testers or the sound of people speaking through their nose.

There's much, much more…

- A *bon vivant* lifestyle – the French live life to the full
- Short working hours (not to mention 11 public holidays per year)
- 2-hour lunch breaks
- A laid back and slower pace of life (if I was any more relaxed, I'd be dead)
- Community values
- Great climate (depending on where you are)
- Romantic Paris - with its galleries, unique cafés and atmosphere is one of the most unforgettably beautiful cities on earth
- The charm of rural France and its glorious, wild-herb covered landscape
- The warm weather laziness of the South
- Lavender-scented Provence
- The food (superb restaurants and fresh, mouth watering market produce)
- Endless feasts, fairs and festivals
- The wine (frighteningly good and way too affordable)
- An unrivalled top class health care system
- Cultural diversity
- A stunningly beautiful language
- Good property bargains
- Location: getting in and out of France is easy and offers a variety of options, including planes (31 regional airports in total), trains, automobiles, boats and ferries

- Little discrimination between young and old. This was a major thing I noticed; when you go to a bar or café in Australia for instance, there are places inhabited by the old and others by the young. This is totally irrelevant here. Old and young mix freely.

> "France is the most civilized country in the world and doesn't care who knows it."
>
> (John Gunther)

La Belle Vie

The first thing one notices about France and the French is their civilized approach to living. A slower pace of life highlighted by different sets of priorities. People don't rush around, angst-ridden and stressed. Sure they have to work to pay the bills like everyone else, but they don't live to work. And one gets the impression they don't need to work to live well.

When one hears stories about the bad customer service in France, I think this is why. Simply speaking, the 'bad' customer service revolves around the de-stressed French mind-set. Next time you wait 30 minutes to be served in a café, don't take it personally. Rest assured the waiter isn't wasting a moment's thought on you.

Beauté

When we think of France it's easy to forget the country's vast diversity. From the wild Pyrenees and snow covered Alps…the rugged expanses of sea to the sexy French Riviera. From endless pastures and charming fairytale villages to Paris, the city of lights, the country really does offer an all-round attractive escape package.

Each season, a self-contained wonder…

Autumn (my favorite), when the country is ablaze with rust colored leaves. When they harvest the grape and numerous seasonal festivals abound.

Winter, when the tourists are gone and you get to hibernate in cosy sweaters and drink red wine by the roaring fire (electric heater in my case).

Spring with its red, yellow and lavender colored wildflower blossoms. Trees covered in pink and white. Bright yellow mimosas veiling Provence like a soft, scented carpet.

Summer. Long, lazy meals spread across rustic tables brimming with local produce. Goodies one picks up at the fresh outdoor markets bustling with people…flower stalls….and men playing *boules* nearby in the late-afternoon light - that famous magic light that's too good not to paint, and precisely the reason why artists have flocked here for centuries.

As if you need more convincing, but hey, just in case…

Inspiration

How about the masses of olive tree groves, a typical landscape staple in the rugged landscape of Provence, immortalized by Cezanne and Van Gogh…the soft scent of wild, ripe figs emanating from the edge of the road, tempting you to pluck them straight from the tree. The sound of cicadas softly chirping in the background - a free, daily concerto.

Liberté

People are alive here; they look at one another, they make eye contact, they appreciate the opposite sex and are not afraid to let it be known. Don't take offence. Even if you stride down the street with your partner, people will look. Men and women alike will check each other out, regardless of age, size, shape, package or color. Minor details are irrelevant here. When it comes to admiring the species of the opposite sex, there is no such thing as discrimination or discretion.

This can be a little intimidating at first but you'll soon get used to it. Perhaps you'll even learn to appreciate it, especially if you are of a certain age. Let's face it; in most other parts of the world, any woman (or man for that matter) past the age of 30 is invisible. Know what I mean?

Not so in France…

Here, people are in touch with their bodies. They are comfortable in their own skin. This can be good and bad. Good because it's refreshing and bad as it makes you feel like you're having a permanent 'out of your own body' experience and that you may never find your way back (unless perhaps a French person shows you the way ;)

If you're not used to it, experiencing this kind of attention can make you feel like a first time visitor - not only to the country but also to yourself. It can feel threatening. Not because the French are a stunningly beautiful race. *Au contraire*. But what they lack in stature they make up in confidence, which is why we're intrigued.

> "Our life is frittered away by detail…simplify, simplify."
>
> (Henry David Thoreau)

Simplicité

One often hears of the French having an appreciation for the 'finer things in life'. Though I'm not sure 'finer' is on the mark. From where I stand, it looks more like an awareness of the 'simple' things. The everyday.

Improvised picnics in parks, smooching with one's sweetheart by the Seine…romantic strolls along cobbled streets, an aperitif on the harbor… open-air street markets, fresh flowers, fruits and vegetables, seafood.

Then there are the national institutions, the cafés or nerve centers from which everything lingers. Here's where you eat, drink, read, write, sit and dream or have impromptu chats with strangers with whom you flirt, philosophize or talk garbage. Who cares, it's probably one and the same. Before his death, Jean-Paul Sartre, the French existentialist and philosopher was famously quoted as saying that everything he'd ever written was a pile of crap.

La Bouffe

In France, the major drawing cards have always been the food, the wine, and of course the cheese. Living here means eating well and taking your time to enjoy the food. Taking pleasure in good food is in fact a ritual and a celebration of life. Since moving to this country, my whole attitude towards food has changed. For one, I now have a downright appreciation for all things fresh. I've turned into a bit of a foodie and a 'slow foodie' at that. No longer eating for the sake of eating, I eat for the experience. To savor the tastes. I have fallen (hopelessly) in love with all of it, from the shopping to the chopping to the serving and the eating.

At first I started taking photos of the food we eat (and other stuff too), simple meals; nothing complicated and created a food/lifestyle blog nobody read. No matter; I did it for my own amusement - as a way of recording tiny moments. A life-stream of sorts.

Art

Another good reason as to why people flock here are the arts. Theater and film are revered and French cinema, also known as "The 7th Art" is taken pretty seriously. The films tend to be character/story driven as opposed to heavy on special effects.

Performing arts aside, there's the fashion, *haute couture*, the architecture and museums such as the *Musee du Louvre* in Paris, one of the largest and most visited museums in the world. In Paris alone, lovers of art have around 40 choices to while away the afternoon.

Once you leave Paris, there are 100 or so more to choose from throughout the rest of France.

The Louvre alone contains 35 000 works of art including the enigmatic Mona Lisa and graceful sculpture of Venus de Milo. Collections include paintings, sculpture, drawings and prints. There is simply no way you can visit the entire museum in one day. If you're a serious art lover, you'll need at least a few days to explore this place, which is housed under a glass pyramid in the former Royal Palace.

If 19th century French art is your passion, then the *Musee d'Orsay* is the place. Focusing on paintings, drawings and sculpture, the collections include impressionism, post-impressionism, realism and art nouveau – all housed in a turn-of-the-century Beaux–Arts classical style railroad station.

To see what I mean, search the Internet for 'museums in France' (by location). You'll need to click on the individual region, then the department:

Architecture

Fabrice and I (used to) live in the 2nd arrondissement of Marseille. Not the best area in town (although it's improving), but it is central and we have a great view across 1800's Haussmann-style buildings framed by the Mediterranean Sea.

The buildings have typical balcony façades and floor to ceiling windows surrounded by thick walls cut from stone.

They are of the same height and roofs are standardized which gives them that well-known prestigious appearance. I never get bored when I gaze through the window or stroll down the street because the ancient architecture ads character, ambience and inspiration to my daily life. Every day I notice something new. A little something I'd never spied before. Like the intricate detail of a wrought iron balustrade. A tiny side street in the Old City. A carefully cultivated patch of green and color on someone's balcony. Antique, wooden hand-carved entrance doors. (I *also* used to take photos of doors because I'm drawn to the idea of portals being magical thresholds where two worlds meet. The public and the private).

Passion

If I had to think of one word to describe France and the French alike, that word would be 'passionate'. The French know how to live and what's needed (and not needed) in order to live this way. To them, it's all about quality of life and the little things, which ultimately (for the rest of us) are the major points of seduction.

Plainly, it is precisely those 'little things' that attract 80 million visitors to France each year. They come, hoping that the French *joie de vivre* will somehow rub off on them. And sure, one gets a taste of it while on vacation, but in order to experience the real thing, *mes amis*, you'll have to live here.

I'm imagining that right about now, you're probably ready to know exactly how to do that.

Let us begin by climbing the biggest mountain.

Visas, Cartes De Sejours/Residency Permits and Work Permits

A lot of people want to come to France and hopefully stay for obvious reasons. It's not easy, France is concerned about immigration numbers, cracking down on things and making the dream a little less accessible.

Notice I didn't say impossible?

Reason being, many people come here from poorer countries. They enter the country legally and illegally putting a strain on social services. Simply put, high unemployment means the government prefers to give its jobs to French citizens.

That being said, let's take a look at how you can stay and work in France.

Visas

Reading about your visa options on the Internet is enough to make your head spin. It's difficult to know where to start, what to believe and where to turn. Official government websites can be even more confusing. Some are in English, some not. Rest assured, I know how you feel, and I will attempt to simplify the maze as best I can.

To begin with, there are two types of Visas:

The tourist visa (short-stay: less than 3 months)

Visa de long séjour (long-stay: over 3 months)

Note: You must apply for the visa de long sejour (long-stay visa) at the French Embassy in your country of residence.

The Tourist Visa

Most visitors are granted an automatic 3 month short-stay (tourist) visa upon entering France. Some countries need to apply for their visas from home so make sure you check with authorities before you go.

In theory, as a visitor, you're expected to adhere to the 'Schengen-rule', which means you need to leave the Schengen area, which currently comprises 26 European countries, after a period of 90 days. For an updated list of Schengen countries you'll need to check the Internet.

In other words, you're not allowed to stay for more than 3 months per 6 months. Who knew??? Like I said 'in theory', once the 3 months is up, you are supposed to leave and wait/stay 3 months in a non-EU country before you can re-enter.

That's a lot of theory for most, which is why some people use the tourist visa to bypass French bureaucracy. They move to France without the long-term visa, pop across the border every few months to get their passport stamped, work under the table and/or live on savings.

Due to lax security at borders, one can sometimes get away with it and plenty of people do but it's absolutely illegal, not to mention incredibly stressful, and you'll never be able to do things like open a bank account, get access to health benefits and such. Plus if you get caught you will jeopardize any future possibility of living in France legitimately. So be careful.

I discovered the 'Schengen rule' by accident when browsing the Internet for some long-stay information. At that stage, I had no idea that I was in fact overstaying my official welcome.

Not knowing what to do, we headed to the local prefecture to ask about our options.

The woman behind the counter asked if I was working in France. I said no. She then told me there was no problem with my staying, unless I was 'using the system' so to speak. Granted she was busy on the day, and I was wearing an extremely cute hat, but what she told me was absolutely the wrong information; I only wish I got her on tape to prove it.

Like I said, I'm certainly not advocating that people stay illegally - and in the long run that's not the answer. I'm saying don't stress too much over the details. Fabrice used to tell me this time and time again. Back then, I didn't believe him, but I have to admit he was right (for once :)

Visa Categories

Before you apply for your cartes de séjour (residency permit), you need to know that there are many different categories:

- **Visiteur:** for people who have no intention of finding work and have enough money to support themselves for one year and/or for people who have PACSed and can't prove they've been living together for at least a year (see below for details)
- **Salarié:** for work contracts (one year or more)
- **Travailleur Temporaire:** if you have a short-term work contract for France (up to one year)
- **Membre de famille:** for family members of someone who already has a carte de séjour
- **Vie Privée et Familiale:** for people married to an EU citizen (see below for more details)
- **Assistant Lecteur/ Visiteur:** for English teaching assistants and/or university lecturers
- **Etudiant:** for students (see below for more details)

- **Scientifique:** for scientific researchers and university professors
- **Profession artistique et culturelle:** for artists and writers
- **Union Européenne:** for EU passport holders
- **Compétences et talents:** Skills and talents card (see below for details) - valid for 3 years (renewable)
- **Carté de Résident** / Resident Permit – valid 10 years (renewable)
- **Retraité / Retirement** – valid 10 years (renewable)
- **Students** (*Etudiants*)

If you'd like to study in France, you apply and the school accepts you, plus you have the necessary funds (around $600 per month) the school can help you to obtain the visa. With a student visa you can apply for a temporary work permit which allows you to work for a limited amount of hours per week/month. A lot of students tend to find work as an *au pair* or in a café/bar/restaurant.

Vie Privée Et Familiale CDS

Since January 1st, 2007, foreigners who receive a vie privée et familiale CDS (for people married to a French and/or EU citizen) have to sign a contract "Contrat d'accueil et d'intégration" and attend a 'welcome to France' orientation. Having said that, some prefectures require it and some don't. Yours truly had to do it :) The deal included 2 days of French history lessons (with free lunch), a French test (short, friendly chat) and the option of 200-400 hours of free French lessons.

Applying For Your Carte de Sejour (Residency Permit)

Once you have your long-stay visa, you'll need to apply for a carte de séjour, (your year-long residency permit) as soon as you arrive in France. When applying, you'll need to supply the following:

- Your visa number
- Date of entry in France (or Schengen area)
- Your address in France
- A copy of passport ID pages and stamp you received upon entry to France
- Your passport
- Proof of accommodation in France
- A passport photo
- Payment for processing (in the form of stamps purchased at a Tabac/ newsagent)
- Fees (at the time of writing) are roughly €55 for students, €70 for salarié, and €340 for

visitors/conjoint de français. Fees vary and change, so make sure to check the form for details

You then have to attend a complete medical examination (by a doctor at the OFII), before you can obtain the highly prized card, which can take 4 - 8 weeks to process. While you wait for the card, you will receive an "attestation" that you have applied, after which your will receive a temporary card called the "récépissé de demande de carte de séjour" - valid for 3 months until you get the *real* carte de sejour/ residency permit.

Note: As aforementioned, you will need to apply for the visa de long sejour (long-stay-visa) from your country of residence, before you come to France. Don't do what I did and think you can apply for the CDS via France. You can't. Not even if you're married to a French citizen (cost me a fortune in plane tickets to find out). Also, allow a minimum of 6 months of pre move 'to-do's'. A year is probably best.

PACS (ing)

"In France, a pacte civil de solidarité (English: "civil pact of solidarity") commonly known as a PACS /paks/ (or PaCS, and now also pacse, is a form of civil union between two adults (same-sex or opposite-sex) for organizing their joint life. ..." (source : wikipedia)

Applying for the Carté de Sejour Visiteur (due to being PACsed)

You are eligible for the CDS Visiteur:

If you have enough money to support your stay in France.

If you are PACSed with your partner and can't prove that you've been living together for at least a year (before you PACSed).

Required documents for the Visiteur CDS (due to being PACsed):

- Passport with visa
- Your French partner's ID card
- Birth certificate, no more than 3 months old
- Certified French translation of birth certificate
- 3 or 4 passport photos (check whether they want black & white or color as it varies)
- Justificatif de domicile (proof of residence in France), such as latest bills with both partners' names on the bill
- A record of your partner's income (3 months worth of pay slips)
- PACS certificate (less than 3 months old)
- PACS contract

Compétences et Talents CDS

The Compétences et Talents/ Skills and Talents card is a (3 year, renewable) residency card - a fairly new loophole for eligible applicants who can - or are seen as contributing to France's development in any of the following areas:

- Economic
- Cultural
- Intellectual
- Scientific
- Athletic
- Humanitarian

This could be you if…

- You are a university graduate
- A qualified professional
- An investor in an economic project
- An independent professional (artist, author, athlete etc)
- A high-end executive or senior manager

Surely you can think of something that fits???

Check the links for more details (the second is in French):

http://www.consulfrance-washington.org/spip.php?article519

https://www.service-public.fr/particuliers/vosdroits/F16922

Carte de Sejour Renewal Process

Ok, so now you've got that darned residency card. What happens next?

Each year (for the following 5 years) you need to jump on the renewal process circuit 2-3 months before your card expiry date. Good news is after 5 years, you can apply for a 10-year residency permit or go for citizenship; it's up to you. (I opted for the 10 years because I needed a break from the paperwork fiasco. In a couple of years when I've recovered I'll probably go for the citizenship. Maybe).

Personally I'm undecided as to whether or not I actually need the citizenship. On the one hand I get exactly the same rights as a resident without being forced to sing 'La Marseillaise', (the French national anthem) during the citizenship ceremony. *Mon Dieu!*

On the other hand, if I ever wanted to live/work elsewhere in the EU, a French citizenship/passport would entitle me to do so.

Depending on your personal, work situation and location, the above reapplication process can vary. Paris is different from Marseille for example. What's more, these things change at the drop of a hat, so always check and confirm with the nearest French Embassy or Consulate.

Some light entertainment…

Here's what happened when I recently renewed my residency permit…

(Excerpt from my diary)

"My temporary residency card (Récépissé de demande de titre de séjour) was about to expire. I went to immigration this morning asking why I never received a renewal notice. They said they contacted me twice over the past 2 months (via mail) but that I had neglected to respond. Not true, I told them. I'm always home, and never received anything via mail.

Needless to say it was my word against theirs…

If my French were better, I would have defended myself in fine form (after being screamed at by the huffing and puffing, red-faced Amazon behind the glass). I would have 'let her have it' with my 'Serbian viper tongue', (Fabrice's loving sentiment whenever I express a hard-nosed opinion).

Now, I am required to cue on Monday for another 4 hours with paperwork to verify I actually live at this address. No problem but it's obvious I'm being penalized because of their negligence. This kind of thing happens a lot I'm told - especially when they're running behind schedule…"

In retrospect, one can only laugh about these things, otherwise nobody in their right mind would live here and be treated in such a manner.

My advice – not *if*, but *when* it happens to you: Take a deep breath, process, accept and get over it.

And remember the following:

When they say it's in the mail, it's not.

When they say you'll receive it by such and such date, you won't.

When they tell you to wait for the call, don't wait because the call will never come.

When they say it's black, assume it's white.

Always get a second opinion on 'advice' given to you by an 'expert'.

Last but not least, don't take anything for granted - go and ask what's going on before the card expires.

Keep in mind you're already in the country. You're here legally and if they are not doing their part on time, that's not your fault. Providing you do it all by the book. As a backup, it's a good idea to keep a note of dates and when you did XYZ and/or sent off papers to XYZ and/or sent emails to XYZ, and that way you have proof. Proof is good. It means they can't kick you out. Better still, it means being able to prove that you are in the right and they are in the wrong. Happiness, my friends!

Phew!!! Needed that.

Retiring in France

From my understanding, it's pretty easy to retire in France. You will need around $1425 to $3725 per month to live here. That's approximately €1055- €2760, depending on your lifestyle and financial situation.

You will be taxed on your US/ overseas pension in France (but there won't be any double-taxation). Before you go, speak to a financial expert and work out the best strategy for you. Once you've established your finances, you can apply for residency.

What you need to apply:

- Request a long-term visa (visa de long sejour - Retraité) at the French consulate office
- Provide the required paperwork
- Provide proof of income (bank account statements, pension statements)
- Proof of health insurance – (Once you're a resident and/or citizen you'll be covered under France's universal health care system - no need to pay extra insurance as it generally doesn't increase the amount of care or benefits you receive. Although it's fine if you want a private room in a hospital etc).

For more information about residency in France for non-EU citizens, check out the following link:

https://www.angloinfo.com/france/how-to/page/france-moving-residency-non-eu-citizens

How to work in France

EU citizens can live and work in France without anybody's permission. For anyone else, here's what you need to do:

- Find a job (if you're lucky the company does all the paper work for you)
- Obtain a work permit (the job is a pre-requisite to getting the permit)
- Apply for a visa de long sejour
- Get on a plane and go to France
- When in France with the visa de long sejour, you can apply for your carte de sejour (local residency/work permit), which you renew on a yearly basis

As already mentioned, due to a relatively high unemployment rate, getting your hands on a work permit is no easy task. Obviously France prefers to give the work to its own citizens (next in line are EU citizens), before they hand a job to a foreigner.

However, if you happen to be working for a company that has branches in France or you work in a specialized field where there are not enough Europeans to do the job, you're in luck. In any case, you or your company will have to prove that you're the best person for the job (meaning better than any European person).

For more information on any of the above check out my favorite (user friendly) site:

https://www.angloinfo.com/france/how-to/france-working

Moving right along…

Embassies and Consulates

Embassy of the United States in France

https://fr.usembassy.gov/

The British Embassy in France

http://www.ukinfrance.fco.gov.uk/en/

Consular services for Australians

http://www.france.embassy.gov.au/pari/consular.html

Canadian Embassy in France

http://www.canadainternational.gc.ca/france/index.aspx?view=d

New Zealand Embassy in France

http://www.nzembassy.com/france

Official French Websites (mostly all in French)

French Office for Immigration and Integration

http://www.ofii.fr/

Official Site for French Administration

http://www.service-public.fr/

Tip: In France, when dealing with consulates, embassies, visa issues etc, check out if you can contact the relevant departments via phone and/or online. If you can, it may save you some major hassle, plus it's a lot more user-friendlier than standing in mind-numbingly dull cues for hours on end.

Marrying a French Citizen

Marrying a French citizen may to some seem like the easiest and most ideal option. Do not be misguided. France is the only country in the EU whereby marrying one of its citizens does not automatically guarantee you citizenship. Yes, you can live and work here once you get married, but you still have to jump through the hoops (as I'm currently doing). And you still have to apply for the appropriate visas from home.

You can opt to get married in France (on a tourist visa). We, however, decided against it because either way, married or not, I would have had to fly back to Australia to apply for the 'visa de long sejour' - which would then entitle me to apply for the 'carte de sejour vie privée et familiale' (the partner/family residency card).

Getting Married in France

In case you've always dreamt of saying 'oui' in France, you will need the following documents:

- Birth Certificate
- ID Card or Passport
- A declaration by your future husband/wife of their domicile, place of residence AND he/she must state in writing that he/she is in fact single (always good to know)
- Names, ages, professions and domiciles of your intended witnesses
- The foreign spouse must provide a birth certificate (translated by a sworn translator)
- A list of witnesses (you'll need at least 2), which is issued by the local town hall

Note: Contact your nearest consulate for specific requirements (as per your individual nationality)

Marrying your French Partner in your Country of Residence

To make a very long story short, we got married in Australia. (It was summer in Australia at the time, so for us it was a no-brainer). To get married on my home turf, all Fabrice needed was: His passport and a current birth certificate translated into English. Easy.

Once married…

We went to the French Embassy in Sydney with the required documents. They then had to validate the marriage in France (just because it's legal in Australia doesn't automatically make it legal in France).

After 4 weeks or so, I received my visa de long sejour and our Livret de Famille - this is a small booklet you receive when you get married in which they record the names of your children and names of your parents in law etc. (Keep the booklet in a safe place because you'll need it down the track).

In Australia, the whole process from wedding to visa took around 6 weeks (they say give yourself 2 – 3 months). Time frames vary depending on your case and which country you're applying from.

How To Become A French Citizen

Although I'm told it takes a long time and feels like never-ending frustration, stress, confusion and out of control spinning round in circles, (while snapping at one's tail), becoming a French citizen is do-able. What's more, if you want to become a French citizen you won't have to worry about losing your original nationality. Dual nationality is accepted.

Rules vary based on individual circumstances, but here are the basic requirements. If at least ONE of the following pertains to you, you're in luck. If not, it doesn't mean this is the be all and end all...

You're in luck if :

- One of your parents is French and/or has French citizenship
- If you're married to a French person and you can prove that you've been married for 5 years. Some say it's one year, but that's a bunch of baloney because the nice woman at immigration told me otherwise
- If you're married to a French person plus you've had a child together (before or after the marriage)
- If you have lived in France for (at least) five years

Once you've determined whether or not you are eligible, you'll need to meet all the following requirements:

- You have to be at least 18 years of age
- You have to prove that you're a good upstanding person
- You must prove that you have no criminal record
- You need to prove that you've integrated well, i.e. that you can speak the language well enough to function in day-to-day proceedings

If things are looking pretty cushy so far you'll then need to put together a dossier, which includes:

- Your birth certificate
- Any other form of identification
- Proof of your marital status (and whether or not you have children)
- Employment records
- Evidence of residence in France
- An 'attestation de moralité', which proves you are of good character

What's next? You wait.

The entire process can take anything between one to two years. At some stage (during your wait), you'll be required to attend a police interview to further determine whether or not you're a 'good quality' future citizen. Too, at some point you'll need to show up at the Tribunal d'Instance to sign a 'request for citizenship' in front of a judge.

How to Integrate

(even if you don't feel like it)

So you've finally got your residency permit and nobody can kick you out. Good. What now?

When you move to a new place, wanting to belong and integrate is one way of doing things. The other way is to not bother, and do your own thing. Everyone's different and not everybody is a social beast. I know I'm not and that's fine by me. If you don't swing that way naturally when you're at home you're less likely to do so when you move overseas.

For those of you who prefer an active social life, I do in fact have a couple of pointers. How is this possible? Well, once upon a time I used to swing that way too. Ironically the more I traveled, the more inward looking I became. Moving around a lot tends to unveil the real you (as opposed to the person you think you are). I discovered I'm basically a traveling shut-in (makes no sense, I know) who on occasion experiences moments of wild abandon.

Your first few weeks in France are likely to be a mixture of excitement and fear. The excitement of being in new surroundings where everything looks different, smells different, sounds and feels different, mixed with the fear of not being sure how to 'be', how to behave out of your comfort zone. I'm afraid that kind of stuff goes with the new territory and all those 'unhinged' feelings are completely natural in your adjustment period until you get used to the place, which (in my humble opinion) can take anything between 6 months to 3 years.

For those who want to **blend as soon as possible, don't hide.** You need to get out there. Start integrating, meeting people and practicing your French. Goes without saying that your new neighbors will be intrigued and are probably dying to meet you. In fact it's a good idea to introduce yourself to your neighbors as soon as you move in. Maybe invite them for a casual apéritif one evening. Unless you have a more creative idea, alcohol and food is still by far the best icebreaker.

Keep up with your old interests and hobbies; once you find your tribe so to speak, it'll be easier to relate to people. Join a yoga class, play tennis, golf or do whatever you used to do. It's also a good time to try something new. Take a local cooking class, learn to paint or enrol in a French course and practice the lingo with people who are in the same *bateau* as you.

The above is probably one of the most important points. Because my husband is French I made less of an effort to create a network of my own, which is fine but it also meant not being able to speak the language as fast as I could have, because I became entirely reliant on him. This, however, made me feel 'heavy' like a ball and chain. Not a nice feeling. So it's best to get out there from the start no matter how intimidating it seems.

Start small. When you buy your baguette in the morning say hello, chat to people, look out for local signs to fetes or concerts. There's a fete just about every week, the French will turn the opening of an envelope into a celebration. Take advantage of this. Buy your fresh produce at the local markets; visit the weekend antique markets and festivals. The more you, do, the quicker you'll assimilate.

What's more, when you **go back to the same places**, be it cafés, pubs, markets, eventually the people will realize you're not a tourist and start to say hello and treat you differently. Suddenly you'll notice that your portion sizes and quality of food (not to mention service) in restaurants are better. I actually never cottoned on to this until my husband pointed it out; but it's true, the more you head back to the same places the better things get.

If you can manage it, just as soon as you arrive, stop converting currencies and **stop comparing things to home.** It doesn't make sense to do so. The faster you accept the vast differences the faster you'll become familiar with your new home. I don't see the point in living somewhere new and still doing the maths in terms of how much a cup of coffee costs compared to home. You'll do it of course, but don't get hung up on it. You'll soon see that everything is relevant.

Integration is not easy. In the beginning, you're likely to speak only to your partner with perhaps an occasional (atrociously pronounced) 'merci' thrown at the supermarket cashier. What's more, it's not plausible to start befriending every person that speaks English. Why not? Most likely that'll be the only thing you have in common, that's why. But beggars can't be choosers and when you feel that sense of isolation creeping in, any company is better than none.

Try and use local artisans for your household/renovation needs. Your community will appreciate it and often you'll find somebody on the cheap. Word-of-mouth recommendation is by far the best way to go. Not necessarily someone out of the local yellow pages.

Join a local class. No matter how small the village, there is bound to be an adult education class or workshop you can join. Even if it's a subject you have no idea about, at least you'll meet people and locals alike. Think dance clubs, sports clubs, martial art, yoga, the gymnasium, swimming pool, cooking class, walking groups etc.

"Man cannot discover new oceans unless he has the courage to lose sight of the shore."

(Andre Gide)

Chapter 2
Practicalities

The Cost Of Living

How much does it really cost to live in France comfortably? Although highly subjective, this question is frequent and fundamental, so I'll do my best to answer it. But first, let's examine what comfortable means to you because your lifestyle will ultimately determine the amount of Euros you'll need to live in France. Think about the following:

- What's important to you?
- What are your values?
- What makes you happy?
- What kind of life do you see for your self /your family?
- What are your plans, dreams, hopes and aspirations?
- Do you really need a car?
- Will you require a mortgage?
- Do you even want a mortgage?
- Do you want to own your home or rent?
- What kind of home?
- Do you have credit card or any other debt?
- Do you really need cable? A television?
- Do you really need the latest 'smart' phone/laptop/gadget/pair of shoes?
- Do you love your work/job? (If yes, could you do the same type of work overseas? If no, what would enable you to do something you not only like, but also love to do? What makes your heart sing?)
- Do you want to start your own business or work for someone else?

As aforementioned, sometimes it takes a while to find out what you really want and who you really are (as opposed to who you think you are). We're not talking about the person that's been created in the eyes of others. We're talking about the real you.

Some people know from day one. Others never find out and there are others still, people like me, who find out somewhere around the halfway point. Never mind I say, better late than never.

Finding the real you is at the center of this whole thing and intrinsic to your happiness, which is fundamentally based on the life you create/unfold for yourself.

For example, back in the old days, when all I wanted to do was work as an actor, I quickly got used to living frugally because I had no choice. From cooking and eating at home to doctoring myself via studying alternative health methods. From choosing picnics and walks as a means of entertainment to buying furniture and clothing in thrift shops. I lived this way for years and I still do. Looking back, I now see my previous situation as a gift because it taught me my most important life lesson so far:

Cutting back and simplifying is not about hardship; ultimately, it's about your freedom and enriching your life. By stripping away the unnecessary and the artifice, by peeling away the layers, eventually you get to find out what's real, what matters, and who you really are.

In hindsight, not having any form of regular income forced me to become a minimalist while simultaneously engaging my imagination and creativity. **In other words, I learned how to practice the art of living well on a small income**. I'm truly grateful for that, and for discovering this way of being long before the current global recession and/or before it became fashionable to do so. Yes, you heard right. Minimalism, and simplicity is the new 'cool'. Trends aside, I honestly believe that simple living (and seeing life through the eyes of the heart) is the ultimate path towards happiness and freedom.

Seriously, if I ever win the lottery (not likely, as you have to be in it to win it), I wouldn't change a thing about the way I live. I'm always amazed (but not surprised) to hear about people who've won the big bucks only to lose the entire gamut within a year. Millions! How is that even possible when one could easily live off one million dollars for the rest of one's life?

If you shoved one million dollars into a 5 percent high interest account (and didn't touch it), you would earn around $50 000 annually in interest, which is more than enough to live the life of your dreams wherever you choose to do so. Food for thought, no?

So why don't people do it? Because they live beyond their means. Because they continue to buy stuff they don't need. Big stuff. Big houses, cars, LCD screens, suitcases full of 'designer label' clothing. They would rather spend their money on things, and vacation only once a year if that. Which would you prefer? More money or more free time? I'm sure you'd agree most people trade their lives for money.

But I'm sidetracking…

Back to France. Tourists often freak out over the prices here and it stands to reason. Why? Because they are referring to 'tourist prices'. As a tourist you will get charged top dollar no matter where you go. And this can leave a bitter taste and lasting impression. Fortunately this impression is not always a correct indicator of how things work – something you can't possible know until you've actually lived in a new place for a while.

On average, it costs a lot less to live in France than Australia, the US, UK and many other European nations. And if you're into statistics you might be interested to know that currently France sits at number 18 on the 'Global Retirement Index' for cost of living.

Clearly, it's cheaper to live in the country or a village than in a city, however, my current home; the city of Marseille in the south of France is still inexpensive.

I believe Marseille and surrounding areas are one of the last truly affordable places in Europe. And I'm not the only one. Since writing the article 'Living in Marseille' for EscapeArtist, I've been inundated with questions about real estate, prices, and everything else.

Paris prices (which are similar to New York prices) and provincial prices vary greatly. Even within Paris, where accommodation prices are approximately 36 percent higher than in regional parts, it depends on which district or arrondissement one is talking about, i.e. central Paris verses the outskirts etc. Having said that, you'll find that prices in Paris are still significantly lower than prices in other European cities. Namely Moscow, Geneva, Zurich, Copenhagen, Milan, London, Bern, Rome and Vienna. Living in France is still approximately 20-25 percent cheaper than living in the UK.

How cheap? With a wide choice of excellent produce available, top quality food and drink need not cost more than €100 per week for 2 people. We mostly eat fruits, vegetables and grains with a little bit of meat. Wine lovers can buy highly drinkable bottles of wine for as little as €5 - even organic wine (there's no way you'd get the same quality of wine in Australia for less than $25 Australian dollars - non-organic). For those still puffing on ciggarettes (like most French people), they cost around €7.00. Eating out doesn't have to break your budget either, especially if you order the fixed price menu starting at €9. When my husband is away I can survive comfortably on €20-30 per week by shopping at local markets. Incidentally a baguette costs around €1.

Here's what you can expect to pay per month (on average)

The prices are based on a couple of clowns with no children living in a 45m2, Haussmanian-style apartment in central Marseille (located 10 minutes walk from the port). Prices will of course vary depending on what region you're interested in. And to give you a more rounded idea, I've included things we don't pay, as I'm aware that for some the following items are indispensable.

Rent: On average, it costs around €550 per month for a 40m2 one-bedroom apartment in the center of town. It's not expensive, neither is it cheap, which is why I recommend buying if you're serious about living or investing here. Recently, I saw a 35m2 apartment in downtown Marseille for €45 000. Not huge, but it has loads of character and sits only a few steps from the old port.

Internet, phone and TV package: From €30 per month (not including cable). We use the nationally available Freebox. http://www.portail.free.fr/

For a more detailed explanation in English: http://www.free.fr/assistance/en/

As far as Internet/phone packages go, you'd be hard-pressed to find anything cheaper. For me, the above represents super value because of the free international phone calls alone. Meaning, if you get a landline you won't need to pay anything for a vast majority of international calls to over 100 countries. This way I get to call my mother in Australia any time I want, speak for as long as I want and it's absolutely free.

For the list of free countries click here: http://www.free.fr/freebox/telephone.html. I know, for instance, that the US and UK are definitely on the free list or 'Destinations Incluses'. If, however, the country you'd like to call is not on the free list, see 'Autres Destinations', and you will see that the countries listed here are heavily discounted, including calls to mobiles.

Groceries: Depending on what and how much you eat, on average, an individual can spend around €100 a week on food. We eat well on around €300-350 per month (for 2 people). Supermarkets are obviously more expensive than local markets. However, there are discount supermarkets such as Lidl and Aldi in almost every suburb, where you'll find the exact same produce for half the price you pay in normal supermarkets. You'll find cheaper still, if you do a little research and seek out the nearest farmer's market (20 minutes from Marseille there's a marché paysan at Plan-de-Campagne every Monday, Wednesday and Friday with farmer direct prices).

Electricity: €45 (based on electric heating and hot water system).

Water: €25 on average.

Petrol per liter: Unleaded €1.30 / Diesel €1.10

Road tolls: Depends on the distance covered. Here's an easy way to find out:

http://www.autoroutes.fr/en/routes.htm

Simply…

- Type in your place of departure (e.g. Paris).
- Type in your destination (e.g. Marseille, Rome, Prague etc)
- Type in your preferred route.

What do I mean by the term 'preferred route'?

For instance, you can choose from the Micheline recommended (usually the most expensive), as well as the quickest, shortest, sightseeing, and economical routes, which will then give you a more or less accurate toll price. In most cases you should be able to seek out the alternative routes and do away with paying tolls entirely, or at least reduce them significantly. For example, when driving from Marseille to Paris, there are actually 5 different possibilities. And thanks to the Romans who built a lot of the roads throughout France, there are basically 2 kinds of roads. The national road/ la route national, which is toll free. And the departmental road/ La route departmental, which is a more scenic route but also toll free.

Clothing: Choose from thrift shops (my favorite) to high-end prices. If you want to dress upbeat at the lowest prices, shop in chain stores like H&M and Zara and/or the local Monoprix department stores for fashionable, stylish (albeit more classic) clothing at a reasonable price.

Need some fashion inspiration? My favorite fashion blogs:

Garance Dore – "For fashion minus the clichés"

http://www.garancedore.fr/

Self Service Magazine – "Paris based fashion and cultural biannual"

http://www.selfservicemagazine.com/index.php

The Sartorialist – Not a French blog, but you'll find loads of Paris street-style-fashion photography to inspire you.

http://www.thesartorialist.com/

Isabel Marant – super hip French fashion designer

http://www.isabelmarant.tm.fr/

Furniture: Again, anything goes – thrift shops, antiques, IKEA and high-end designer pieces. Fabrice enjoys making furniture from recycled products. He created our bathroom sink and cupboard from an old industrial washing machine. Our kitchen cabinets are made from recycled teak (old boat materials). Our bedside table is an ex-icebox with legs. All in all, you get a kind of half-boat, half space-ship effect throughout our apartment. Every inch of the apartment is handcrafted, unique and special.

As far as low cost furniture and home appliances, really, your best bet is to surf the local classifieds for privately sold, second hand goods and furniture. Here's a great site that covers all of France:

http://www.leboncoin.fr/

Simple storage items you're better off buying new. Although a lot of historic apartments in France have brilliant features such as floor to ceiling windows and doors, super-high ceilings and plenty of charm, they often lack in storage space, hence, occasionally we shop at IKEA for practical and cheap storage items/furnishings (There are 2 stores in Marseille).

http://www.store-locator.com/en/e-5-7/IKEA_Locations_France/

Cinema ticket: €8 (to avoid nasty voice dubbing; look out for original English language versions of the film, marked as VO (version originale). In Marseille, you'll find them at cinema Variétés near the old port; Adresse : 37, rue Vincent-Scotto (angle Canebiere).

Metro/Bus ticket: €1.50

Sandwich/Baguette with filling: €4.50

Bread/Baguette: €0.90

Restaurant meal: €9-20

Postage Stamp: €0.56

Habitation and Property Taxes: are made up of 2 parts:

Taxe foncière: payable by the owner of the property (the tax is for local council services).

Taxe d'habitation: Payable by the owner or tenant of the property (this tax depends on the size of the place, i.e., the m2 and it includes a tax on TV). All prices depend on the size, condition and location of the property. Prices in small towns or villages are likely to be cheaper than those for cities. An average yearly price would be around €1500. We pay €1400 annually for a 45m2 apartment, including both taxes (taxe fonciére and taxe d'habitation).

House, Car and Health Insurance:

Frankly, we don't deal with any of those (preferring to live dangerously), but here's a link to a reputable company I found via forums. 'Prevencia l'assurance' covers the whole of France and they speak English. Best of all, their prices are comparable to any other French brokers. Further details: http://www.insurance.fr/

Renovations:

If you're considering renovating, things like paint tend to be a little pricy. Power tools are reasonable but smaller fiddly items like screws, nuts and bolts are expensive. It's the same with white goods like fridges and washing machines. If you can be bothered, it might in fact be cheaper to pop across the borders to buy some of these items…though I seriously doubt the difference (which you'll make up in petrol money) is worth the effort, unless you buy a whole gamut of stuff.

As you can see, even on a tiny budget, living in France is still affordable. If you don't have a mortgage, credit card debt or car payments and/or a champagne and caviar lifestyle, you can get by on as little (or less in our case) as €1370 per month (the national minimum wage) which is around $1500 US dollars. Having said that, we have managed on much less, like €600. Microscopic you may think, but I'm simply demonstrating that it's do-able and what's more, it's do-able without feeling that one is missing out on life-quality.

I understand that for some people our lifestyle may not be the best example. We don't have kids. We don't frequent restaurants, fast food places and bars. We eat at home and visit friends, (the preferred way of socializing in France). So for us, it pretty much comes down to groceries and basic bills.

Having little to no overheads is the key here, and for anyone who is not in a similar position, I highly recommend getting rid of all your debts and 'stuff' before you even think of moving.

Easier said than done? Not really. You see, if you're currently paying off a mortgage and feeling trapped because of it (as I was before I left Australia), your current prison could very well be your ticket to freedom. See the **Real Estate** chapter for more details.

Learning The Language

"Never too old, never too bad, never too late, never too sick to start from scratch once again."

(Bikram Choudhury)

A friend of mine said that listening to the French language compares to the sound of birds having a chat. True. The language itself is exquisite to hear and even more fun to speak. For me it's on par with Italian - equally melodic, yet different.

Like it or not, French has influenced English in a huge way. It is already a part of our daily lives, with common terms like *bon voyage, brunette, rendezvous, toilette* just to name a few - in fact, there are many similarities between English and French, including a common alphabet.

Knowing French is a huge asset not only in France. *La belle langue* is spoken on every continent in the world - in fact in more than 33 countries worldwide including Switzerland, Luxembourg Belgium, Canada, the Caribbean, Vietnam, North-West and Central Africa.

Just like Italian, Spanish, Romanian and Portuguese, it is one of the Romance languages, descended from Latin. In addition, the language is widely used in diplomacy, arts and science. And due to it's grammatical precision, it is the official language by major organizations like the OECD (Organization for Economic Corporation and Development).

That being so, naturally France works hard at continuously promoting its language and culture.

Parlez-vous français?

If you already speak the language you're in luck. If not, I suppose in one way you don't need to in order to buy tomatoes and bread but it sure as hell helps.

If you really want to learn, don't despair; there's hope for you yet. How do I know? Because I've been there. And having been there, I am convinced that anyone can learn to speak a new language, at any age, even if they've never studied languages before. What's more, I don't believe that learning a new language is necessarily a cerebral/ intellectual pursuit.

In an attempt to sound semi-lucid, let me try to explain…

If you're an actor, for example, it probably helps to learn your lines, right? Wrong. I never did. Not by rote, that is. The way I was trained was to learn via the body, by moving through the space/ stage and reading the lines out loud. My body would then let me know where I physically needed to be in the space/ or stage.

In other words my body would kinesthetically link up movement and text without me having to 'make a decision'. When it all lines up it's almost like hearing a 'click', but instead of hearing it you *feel* it.

For me, this is (to this day) the easiest way to retain text. Not in my head, but in my body. It then becomes 'body memory' so to speak, and I honestly feel that learning a language can be achieved in pretty much the same manner.

How? Glad you asked. It's really quite simple. Repetition creates body memory. If you repeat something often enough, eventually it stays with you. And if you incorporate a physical action to coincide with the spoken text it works even better.

If you can relate to what I'm saying, then that's great. Most likely it means you're a kinesthetic learner. It means you sense, or feel your way through life. If, however, what I just explained sounds like gobbledygook, you're probably better off learning the language via conventional methods, i.e. by learning all the bells and whistles, including grammar.

This is the third time I've been in this boat. Although born in Serbia, I grew up speaking German in Austria, then English in Australia. Now, at 40-something, I'm learning French.

They say it's easier to learn a language when one is young, and I agree – though not with the intention of dissuading anybody. Quite the opposite. I'm far from being a linguist (not by a long shot), but if you break it all down it comes down to this: Children are like sponges that soak up information. It seems as though they learn via osmosis and/or intuitively. This, I feel, is the natural way to learn. When we grow up, we tend to complicate stuff when we don't need to.

Simplify Your Language Learning

As they say, the best way to learn a language is to immerse yourself in the culture, and if you've read this far you're probably half way there already. Of course once you live in France, you will have no choice but to learn French because you'll be surrounded by it. Even so, it's best to start before you leave home:

- **Contact "Alliances françaises":** http://www.alliancefr.org. If you're not interested in their course, they may still have a couple of tips on the topic.
- **Buy an electronic translator.** You can pick them up via Amazon for around $40. In France it cost me €70. Why the translator?
  They are fast and efficient, like a dictionary but without having to manually find the word.
  They're handy during conversation, when you need to find a word or form a simple sentence quickly.
  They teach grammar via word games.
  They're great to annoy French people with … *"Excusez-moi. Juste une seconde…mais…"*
- Make **"Google Translate"** http://www.translate.google.com/
  your new best friend. To use the (free) online translation service, all you do is copy/paste the French text into the box. Adjust the tabs above the box to 'From French' to 'To English' (and vice versa) to instantly translate text and web pages. Works for most other languages

too. Or else you can manually type in the text and repeat the same procedure. Aside from being a fantastic learning tool, it's a major advantage when you're attempting to read French websites/ documents and you haven't got a clue.

Bear in mind when translating chunks of text and paragraphs, the translation is never accurate (it can't be because a computer can't fully replace a human being – at least not yet) but for short pieces it's absolutely fine. As I said, you won't get an exact translation but you will get the general gist.

> "If you make yourself understood, you are always speaking well."
>
> (Moliere)

If you have cable, listening to and **watching the news in French** is great for getting your ear accustomed to the different sounds. Newsreaders have an annoying way of over articulating, which can actually work for us here. You see, when you first start listening to French it tends to sound like one great big bundle of minced up words but eventually, the more you practice your listening skills, the more you'll be able to hear the words separately, identify commonly used words and even comprehend certain terms.

When In France, **speak!** The best way to practice is by speaking. In France, you'll find French-English Conversation groups (for all levels).

These groups offer formal and informal meetings (if you opt for the informal, there's less pressure about the grammar) and they're the perfect solution for anybody who can't commit to a regular (school) study program. Another bonus is that they are inexpensive and a great way to meet people.

For more information and regular listings, check out: http://www.parisvoice.com

and/or

http://www.fusac.org

For language exchange conversation practice try :

http://www.meetup.com/TalkTime/

or

http://www.parlerparlor.com/

(free-form conversation with native French and English Speakers)

Go ahead and make mistakes! Yes, people will on occasion laugh, but don't take it personally, in fact stop taking anything personally from now on - quite often they laugh because they think your attempts are cute, admirable, charming and/or brave. I used to care but now I don't. Mistakes mean you're improving. Play it safe and you stagnate.

Grammar-phobe? Let it go. The most important thing is to try and communicate. That's the first barrier. I mean everyone is different, but speaking from personal experience, if I allowed myself to get caught up in the grammar straight away, I'd be too scared to open my mouth.

Listen. Remember the bit about learning via osmosis? If you have nobody to listen to, use the TV and watch French films (with or without subtitles); or listen to the radio (which you can also get over the net). My favorites (for eclectic music, talk shows and almost zero advertising) are:

http://www.radiogrenouille.com

http://www.fipradio.fr/

If you make it a habit to turn on the radio while you do the cleaning or whatever, eventually something starts to shift and sink into your sub-conscious. It won't happen over night, but at some point it will.

Read. Everything you can get your hands on. Menus, newspapers, magazines, children's books. You'll be surprised how many French words are already used in the English language. Perhaps that's why we tend to comprehend before we can actually speak. Here's a list of French/English expression:

https://en.wikipedia.org/wiki/List_of_French_expressions_in_English

Schools Verses Self-Taught

Let's face it; some folks are better at learning languages than others. People are generally visual, aural or kinaesthetic creatures (or a combination of all three) and tend to learn accordingly. Some slow, some fast, but it really doesn't matter how long it takes. What matters is working out your personal study goals…

- What level of fluency do you want to attain?
- What's your budget?
- What's your learning style?
- Do you work/study best in a group, one-on-one or by yourself?

…and then finding what works best for you.

Choosing the right school/ course is vital. If the material is too heavy in theory and lacking in everyday speech, colloquialism and vocabulary, you're not doing yourself any favors. Apart from that, sitting in a classroom can feel nauseating (high school was traumatizing enough the first time around, no? :)

Language Schools

Alliance Française (Paris)

http://www.alliancefr.org

France Langue (Paris)

http://www.france-langue.fr

Accord Ecole de Langues (Paris)

http://www.accord-langues.com

Language International (Marseille)

http://www.languageinternational.com/french-courses-marseille-23711

Easy French (Marseille)

http://www.easyfrench.net/

Alliance Française (Marseille)

http://www.orbislingua.com/ebaca146.htm

L'institut Destination Langues (Marseille)

http://www.destinationlangues.com/?lg=en

Links to other language courses throughout France

http://www.europa-pages.com/france/index.html

As an aside: When I lived in Japan I met foreigners who had studied Japanese at their respective universities for years. Apparently (back home), their grammar, reading and writing where spot on but in Japan, when faced with a real-life situation they felt somewhat challenged to say the least. Frankly, the best place to learn French is in France.

Self-Study

- Interested in a **private tutor**?
  Try FUSAC: http://www.fusac.com

or

- The Paris Voice http://www/parisvoice.com
- Check out your local mairie (town hall) for private tutors and individual classes
- **Find a buddy** to practice with
- Sign up for the **online French language newsletter** by Laura K. Lawless. So far, it's the best I've come across. There are hundreds of lessons (for all levels) with tons of valuable information, and it's free! http://www.french.about.com/
- Looking for a creative and productive way to spend your lunch hour? Why not try a free online listening course like **Coffee break French.** The program consists of short 10 – 15 minute French lessons that really pack a punch (includes other languages too). http://www.radiolingua.com/shows/french/coffee-break-french/
- The best home study course I've come across is **Assimil - New French With Ease** (includes 4 audio CD's and a 591 page book). This is the one I use. I like it because it's easy to follow, it touches on grammar without the heavy-handedness, it's fun, inexpensive and it actually works!
  http://www.amazon.com/French-Ease-Assimil-Method-Books/dp/2700520130
- **Fall in love with a French person** (optional, though highly recommended).
- Try to learn a little every day, that way it stays in your subconscious as opposed to going to French class once a week. 5 or 10 minutes per day is better than 2 hours per week. Make it

fun instead of a chore.

Tips for making it fun:

- Watch (bad) French soapies on TV. Why? Because the scripts are always terrible (as in 'the light's on but nobody's home' basic) and they usually don't speak too fast:) Also good for picking up on body language/facial language mannerisms.
- Learn the words to a French song (then you'll know what the hell Piaf was on about)
- Stick yellow **'post it' notes** all around the house. Fridge, door, toothbrush, floor, cupboard, mirror…you get it, right?
- **Learn French Slang** (it's fun and perfect for when you want to impress). Here's a great book for inspiration: http://www.amazon.com/Hide-This-French-Book-Editors/dp/9812464298/
- If you feel **challenged by the pronunciation;** again the easiest way to conquer this is to keep listening to French being spoken. Plus if you think of French names we already use in the English language. Words such as *rendezvous* for example, then the pronunciation issue doesn't seem so huge. Be prepared to screw up and sound ridiculous. After all, everyone was once a beginner.

Point is you need to communicate to integrate; otherwise you'll always feel on the outer. If you take a shot at it, you'll reap rewards. The French will certainly appreciate your efforts and (more often than not) respond warmly. Just in case they don't (respond warmly), ask them if they'd prefer to speak English instead. Ha !

So plunge in. Start today, by memorizing a few key words/phrases, the type of stuff you'll be using everyday. Baby steps, my friends. That's the key.

Hello, Good morning/ *Bonjour*

Goodbye/ *Au Revoir*

Please/ *S'il vous plait*

Thank you/ *Merci*

Good night/ *Bonne nuit*

How much? / *Combien?*

I don't understand / *Je ne comprends pas*

I'll wind up here by letting you in on a little secret: Don't worry about your 'funny accent'. The French love it; in fact they even find it sexy, alluring, and enchanting. You can trust me on that one.

> "Once you learn to let go, things just start to happen"
>
> (Erin Hapta)

Health Care in France

In France one raises one's glass with a pronounced *'A votre Sante'*, which means 'to your health', and just as well. As already mentioned, the French drink a lot of wine, so it goes without saying they need to take their health care seriously.

The French health care system is reputedly one of the best in the world, insuring a high quality of care. This happens because every person working in France is obligated to chip in part of their salary into a state controlled health insurance fund, of which the employer contributes the majority. On average, that's 20 percent of their pay.

I guess that's why the French live such a relatively stress-free existence – (while smoking truckloads of cigarettes and drinking gallons of rosé). They know there's no need to worry about what's going to happen if they need to go to hospital.

70 percent of the costs on average are funded back to the patient. There's a 95 percent payback for major surgery, 80 percent for minor surgery, 95-100 percent for childbirth, 70 percent for X-rays, general dental care and nursing care for home patients. Plus, prescriptions are reimbursed at up to 65 percent (depending on the drugs), although most of them I'm told are free.

> "A hard drinker, being at the table, was offered grapes for dessert. 'Thank you,' said he, pushing the dish away from him, 'but I am not in the habit of taking my wine in pills'."
>
> (Jean-Anthelme Brillat-Savarin)

In France, 99 percent of the population is covered by basic universal health care, an organized health-care system built around the principle of universal coverage for all members of society, making sure that even the poorest people are protected. What's more, most of the population -(84 percent) are satisfied with the quality of treatment. I suppose that's why the French live longer (81 years on average). That's a lot of wine.

Funny, at some point their super-health-care-system must have turned them into a bunch of paranoids who run to the doctor every 5 minutes. For one, they can afford it. If not, there's a chemist/pharmacie on practically every corner (look out for a green flashing cross, can't miss it).

If you're married to a French person the entire family is covered by the French National Health Care System (including children under 18). In case you're wondering about babies, I once read about a woman who'd had twins by caesarean section (she was French, her husband English) and had to spend 9 days in a private room. The first night cost $165 and the rest practically nothing. The bill for 9 days in a private hospital room totalled $190. Evidently, having babies in France is affordable.

What's more, health care is highly socialized. It does not discriminate on income levels so everybody gets treated equally. In an emergency situation for example, there is no way you would be turned away because you don't have the money.

I dare say if you went to the doctor without a penny, you'd also be treated. French Doctors make between $50–100 000 thousand per year. A lot less than in some countries, alas, that is the standard set by their government.

Primarily French doctors see themselves as public servants. Most of them are more than happy with their situation, having studied medicine to actually help the sick and injured. All that with so little pay? Hmmm…

And did you know…

When you call emergency you actually get to talk to a real doctor first, who will then determine the seriousness of the matter. This is time and cost efficient as 60 percent of the cases, they can usually treat via the phone or on the scene. The idea, of course is to bypass the emergency room, which cuts down on costs.

It's true that some people who come to France tend to abuse the system, flocking here in high numbers, often just for the health care alone. Although the country is running at somewhat of a deficit and something will clearly need to be changed in the future, for now the system remains as it is. If not, most certainly the French themselves would have a thing or two to say about it.

Health cover for Residents

If you choose France to call home - as in it becomes your country of residence; you'll automatically be covered. Once you're settled in, you need to subscribe to the French Social Security System, which includes health insurance. Any dependents are automatically covered.

Subscribing to the general French social security system will cover your basic health insurance needs. Part of the medical expenses will be reimbursed but you need to keep the evidence such as prescription labels etc in order to put in your claim.

Coverage - is generally between 60-100 percent, depending on the type of procedure. The French National Health Care System covers most of the costs; private insurance companies pick up the rest.

If you see a doctor it costs around €23 (around 33 USD), of which you get back around €20. Regardless of whether or not you have healthcare in France, anybody can still go to the Doctor but generally, that's how much it'll cost you. I went to the chiropractor a couple of times and paid €25 per visit. An Osteopath costs around €50 for a 40 minute session (not reimbursed).

For information about having a surgical procedure or operation in France contact: http://www.france-surgery.com/en/

For more extensive information on French healthcare including details about:

- Pregnancy and Birth
- Finding a Doctor
- State Health Insurances
- Emergency numbers (who to call and what to say in an emergency situation)

More information here: http://www.expatica.com/fr/healthcare/Moving-to-France-Healthcare-for-expats-in-France_101669.html

Short-term visitors

EU (European Union) citizens are automatically covered (due to reciprocal agreements among EU countries) - meaning all EU citizens are issued the European Health Insurance Card.

Non-EU citizens need to check whether or not there is a bilateral agreement that will cover you in France for limited emergency health care. If not, you are best to get private insurance that covers you in France.

Some well-worn terms

Carte Vitale - is a medical card the French use when they see the doctor. Usually they need to hand over the card and pay up front for which they get reimbursed. The money goes straight into their bank account.

SECU - also referred to as La Sécu or Sécurite Sociale is the acronym for Social Security in France - the government agency that administers health care.

Mutuelle – is the private health cover. It pays for what the SECU doesn't pay – making up the difference and costing on average 80–90 USD per month for a family of three (again, a lot of this is reimbursed). A lot of people tend to go without the Mutuelle. It's up to you to decide whether or not you think it's worth it. I don't have it, nor does my husband. I didn't need it when I went to hospital here (read below) and I still received a high quality treatment without the private health care cover.

How to lose weight French-style

If you happen to be overweight and you want to lose the excess luggage, do it the French way. Brides-Les-Bains, a French version diet-boot-camp (known for its thermal springs in the south-east of France), offers some first-class treatment. Here's what it looks like:

- Thermal waters
- Spa treatments
- Walks
- Sports
- Cooking classes
- A personal dietician to calculate what you need to do to lose weight

Sound good? Here's where it gets even better…

This health incentive by the government for children and adults alike lasts for 3 weeks and is practically FREE (i.e. reimbursed).

Speaking from experience…

Some months ago while waiting for a train in Cannes I felt a little off-color - dizzy, nauseous, and kind of panicky. All I wanted (and could) do was to sit down as fast as I could, so I ducked inside the train station café and ordered herbal tea.

My symptoms progressively worsened. So much so that I'd lost my ability to get up and walk. What's more, I must have been pale as a ghost because at one stage the waiter asked me if I was ok. Oui, oui, I managed on several occasions until finally, I had to admit I wasn't.

Long story short, the waiter called the 'fire department based ambulance' (used for less serious issues). They arrived within minutes and after a brief chat, checked my blood pressure, which was normal. Then, (not knowing what else to do with me), they asked if I would like to go to the hospital for further blood tests. I hesitated. Why? Because I was worried about the 'practicalities'.

"How much will it cost"? I asked the (shockingly handsome) *pompiers* who where somewhat perplexed by my hesitation. Here's what they said…

"Why, you are in France Madame, so it is free".

I knew the general health system was reputed to be good, but I had no idea about specifics. My situation was as such: I was married to a French citizen, yet still not covered under the French Social Security System (Sécurité Sociale) because my husband had neglected to renew his.

No matter. Over the next 4 hours at the hospital I was seen by an English speaking doctor, given an ECG and a general blood test, which further determined there was nothing serious wrong with me, (in retrospect probably just hypoglycaemia).

Ok so now we know that I'm a hypochondriac, but hey, at least I got to be a guinea pig for the book. Lucky for me, my neurotic episode didn't cost an arm and a leg, plus, I received the bill, €170, almost 10 months after the event.

In Australia, without medical insurance one would pay close to $1000 for emergency transport to a hospital and almost $300 for the nice ambulance people to stop by (sans the joy ride to the hospital). God forbid if you end up in emergency. You'd have to sit and wait patiently for several hours (severed arm or not:)

Educating Your Child in France

"The illiterate of the 21st century will not be those who cannot read and write. But those who cannot learn, unlearn and relearn."
(Alvin Toffler)

Schools in France are mostly public. In general, there seems to be less focus on private education because the benefits of a private verses public education seem to be of little consequence (depending on who you talk to and which side of the fence he or she is coming from). Hence, most students go to public school until a University level is reached.

Standards are high and the consistency of standards is evident throughout the country because the children are subjected to the same textbooks and subjects of study at the same time.

Clearly, the system is less 'sports' orientated than in the US and UK and definitely far less than in Australia. Instead, a great part of the learning is dedicated to academics. Unfortunately, long gone are the days when practical skills such as cooking sewing, woodwork, metal work, known as *traveaux pratiques* where given equal weight for children aged 7 years onwards.

Having said that, maybe that's about to change. Recently I noticed a lot of schools fostering their own organic vegetable gardens, encouraging students to participate in the daily care, sowing and harvesting of the crops, thereby instilling practical skills as well as a nutritional education. (Anything that teaches youngsters what a real tomato looks like has to be a good thing).

In France, school is compulsory for children aged between 6 and 16. Generally speaking, in Europe, teaching methods tend to be more rigid. Having grown up in Austria until the age of 12 before immigrating to Australia I can honestly say that in comparison, Australian schools felt like a walk in the park.

For starters, in France and Europe, children are obligated to learn another language. Most learn English; hence most of them understand and speak Basic English.

Even though it may seem like a huge deal to whisk your little ones out of school and stick them into a new school and new country, it really doesn't have to be. Being exposed to different cultures makes kids more resilient. Plus, don't forget there are other expats around who are in exactly the same boat.

Most kids pick up a new language fairly easily. I learnt English in a year. The younger the child, the easier it will be. Most likely, your little angel will speak fluent French way before you do - and probably without an accent.

Nursery School

Although not compulsory, nursery schools are free of charge. Children have to be a minimum of 2 years old and they get to stay in there until their 6th birthday, after which you can register them for primary school. If you're not sure which school, contact the town hall (Mairie) of your place of residence.

To register your child you need the following pieces of paper:

- Your family record book (livret de famille)
- A document stating your child has had all his/her necessary vaccinations, which are compulsory for his/her age group

Note: If you don't believe in vaccinating your child you can get around that with a statement that the vaccinations can't be given for whatever your personal reasons.

Primary School

Primary School is mandatory from age 6 but you need to have registered your child at the beginning of the school year in the same year of the child's 6th birthday. Again, be prepared to produce the papers...

- A registration certificate from the town hall
- Your family record book (livret de famille)
- A healthcare record book to verify your child's vaccinations or an exemption thereof
- If your child can't or is unable to practice sports you need to submit a medical certificate

Secondary Education

In France, secondary education is organized in two phases: The compulsory **Collèges** cater for the first years of secondary education (ages 11 to 14), followed by a second cycle of study at a **Lycée** (ages 15 to 18), where students prepare for the **Baccalauréat**, which can lead to higher education studies. Again, you need to have registered your teenager at the local Mairie by June. For further clarification, check out the following websites:

http://www.expatica.com/fr/education/Education-in-France_101147.html

http://www.Service-Public.fr

For a comprehensive step-by-step guide (in French) to enrolling your child in a school:

http://www.education.gouv.fr/cid37/inscription.html.

Alternative Schooling

Apart from public schools there are plenty of alternatives like International Schools offering an entire curriculum in English, such as American and British schools in Paris that follow the exact US/UK curricula. What's more, there are Bilingual Schools (French and English), with a high level of English taught by native English speaking teachers. For more information contact ELSA (English Language Schools Association) http://www.elsa-france.org/

If none of those options seem right for you and/or your little one, you could always consider home schooling. I don't have kids, but if I did I imagine I'd be heading down that road - mainly because I don't feel a general school system is geared towards *real* learning. It's geared towards rote learning the required information and retaining it long enough for students to regurgitate within a 2-hour examination.

With a bit of luck and/or depending on their rote learning skills, they will regurgitate the right information so they can get the right piece of paper to hang on the wall as a reminder of having learnt something in the first place.

Or, (as is my case) as a reminder of the fact that I still owe thousands of dollars for my education, which I'll be paying off until the day I die. That's if I get a 'real job' in the first place (not likely because I don't want one).

The problem with most school systems is that individual skills are not recognized and/or valued. Your kid could be extremely gifted in one area, like music for example, but if you send her/him to a normal school, chances are the world will miss out on the next Beethoven. What's more, students are not encouraged to think outside the square and/or taught enough practical life skills. If you can afford them, schools like **Montessori** http://www.montessori-paris.com/ or **Steiner** http://www.steiner-waldorf.org/ come closer to what one would imagine to be a good alternative education system. If not, as already mentioned, there's home schooling.

Home Schooling

In France home schooling has been legal since 1998. However, certain standards need to be met so that the level of a home schooling education can be comparable to that of a conventional school education.

The following subjects are required learning:

- Written and spoken French
- French literature
- Mathematics
- One foreign language
- Science and technology (Basics)
- History and Geography of France, Europe and the rest of the world (Basics)
- Artistic education
- Sport

Aside from the above, you are expected to adhere to the following:

- Annual registration is compulsory
- Expect a yearly visit from the school inspector (for children between 6-16)
- Expect a visit from the mairie every two years
- A yearly declaration at the local marie must be made at your place of residence
- National exams to be taken (once registered at the rectorat)
- A yearly declaration must be made at the school inspectorate or inspecteur d'académie

Further information on home schooling available here:

Les Enfants d'Abord

http://www.lesenfantsdabord.org/

Government education website

http://www.education.gouv.fr/bo/1999/hs3/som.htm

General details

- The school year starts early September and finishes for summer holidays in July.
- The school week is 24 hours long.
- School hours are generally between 08.30-16.30 (with two breaks in between).
- Lunch lasts between 1.5 – 2 hours.
- State schooling and books are free but parents are expected to pay for stationery supplies and school outings.
- Required Vaccinations: The Diphtheria-Tetanus-Polio (DTP) is compulsory, and you'll need to present a vaccination certificate upon enrolment. Tuberculosis (BCG) is no longer obligatory since 2007, except under certain circumstances. Again, if you don't believe in vaccinating you could, for example, ask a homeopathic doctor to write you a certificate. An exemption, at least for the (BCG), is acceptable at most schools.

Driving in France

"Europeans, like some Americans, drive on the right side of the road, except in England, where they drive on both sides of the road; Italy where they drive on the sidewalk; and France, where if necessary they will follow you right into the hotel lobby."

(Dave Barry)

I stopped driving some 7 or so years ago when I sold my car in Australia. It was an old FIAT, an acronym that stands for 'Fix It All The Time'. So when I finally got rid of the money guzzler, I thought it was a good time to stop driving altogether. I'm glad I did. Don't miss it one bit, plus, I choose to see the whole thing as my contribution to the environment.

To be perfectly honest, even if I had my local license, I don't think I'd be brave enough to drive here. Statistically speaking, French roads are twice as dangerous as British roads (and probably 3 times as dangerous as Australian roads).

The reasons as to why are too numerous to count, but I'll name a few just off the top of my head…

- Poor or no-existent road signaling.
- Lack of traffic lights (generally, there's one set of lights per junction), making them easy to miss.
- Traffic lights go straight from red to green.
- Traffic regulations enforcement varies between regions.
- Poorly indicated roundabouts.
- Lack of cats-eye markings (not good for visibility especially at night or during bad weather).
- Lack of road markings at junctions.
- Dangerous driving (hairy overtaking maneuvers to say the least).
- Zero driving distance between cars.
- Unfamiliar road signs such as "priorité a droite" (indicated by a black X in a red triangle) – meaning the road joining your road has priority and you need to give way to traffic (even if you're on a major road and the other road is a dirt road). Yep :)
- Different speed limits (max on motorways is 130 km/h, dual carriageways or roads separated by lanes, max is 100 km/h, main roads, non-build up areas max is 90km/h, built-up areas max is 50 km/h.

French road sign vocabulary and images click here:

http://www.france-pub.com/french/french_traffic.htm

and here:

http://www.visitnormandy.wordpress.com/2009/03/25/biker-friendly-bed-and-breakfast-in-normandy-sarthe-french-traffic-signs-highway-code

If the different sets of rules, road rage and general madness aren't enough to put you off, and/or you think I'm over-reacting, read on:

How To Obtain Your French Driver's License

You can get a driver's license from the Prefecture de police within one year of residency in France. In a lot of cases it is a simple exchange for a French license. You can drive with your foreign driver's license for one year in France, after which you'll need to get your French "permis de conduire".

There are 2 ways to do that:

Go to driving school for 2 months and pass a written exam and driving test which costs around €800.

Drive something that doesn't need a license like a moped, microcar or tractor. (See below for details)

What's a Microcar?

Microcars or "*Voitures sans permis* (also known as voiturettes or quadricycles) with a maximum of two seats, an engine size up to 50cc (petrol engines), or maximum power of 1 KW (electric cars) or 4 KW (other forms of propulsion, including diesel), a maximum speed of 45 Km/h, a maximum unladen kerb weight of 350 Kg and a maximum load capacity of 200 Kg..." (source: http://www.angloinfo.com)

Official information (in French) on obtaining your French drivers license:

http://www.mfe.org/index.php/Thematiques/Demarches-administratives/Permis-de-conduire-francais-Echange-a-l-etranger

For detailed information on topics listed below (in English) click here:

http://www.fusac.fr/driving-in-france/

Driving Rules and Regulations

Basically when it comes to driving in France there are 2 sets of rules. The written and the unwritten. I'll start with what's expected, but I'll also give you what I 'see' on a day-to-day basis.

- It is compulsory to carry your driving documents with you in case of spot checks. These include original versions of: Passport, Drivers Licence, Vehicle Insurance, Vehicle Registration and a current MOT certificate (to prove your vehicle met the minimum environmental and road safety standards required). <u>Third party car insurance is compulsory.</u>

- It is compulsory to wear a seat belt (front and rear if fitted).

- Children under 10 must sit in the back and wear a seatbelt especially fitted/adapted for children.

- Don't drink and drive. Most French people do, so it's best to stay ahead of the game.

- Mobile phones are not to be used when driving except a 'hands free' version (again, that's the theory. In reality people do and, yes, I have seen people stopped by the police for doing so).

- Use your headlights when visibility is bad otherwise, driving with lights on during the day is optional.

- You must carry a warning triangle and fluorescent warning jacket in the car (not the boot), which needs to conform to EU standards.

- When crossing a road, pedestrians have priority over cars, provided they clearly indicate their intention with a forward step or a hand gesture (in reality it usually consists of a frantic wave and/or and obscene hand gesture involving the pedestrian's middle finger). If the crossing is less than 50 meters away, drivers are not obligated to yield to pedestrians in any way, shape or form - and usually don't. If you happen to be the pedestrian, remember to signal and cross with confidence. Hesitate and you'll wait until the cows come home.

- Stick to the right! Obvious, I know, but you can always tell foreign drivers and to be honest the locals consider them to be a pain in the derriere because they play it 'too safe', thereby holding up the rest of the traffic that's desperately heading off to lunch, an apéritif, a secret rendezvous with a 'friend'/ mistress - and on rare occasions even home to dinner.

- Remember also to give way to cars on the right (priorite a droite) - in a nutshell this means give priority to motorists turning on to the road you're on from 'your right' (except when you're at a stop sign, at a traffic light or roundabouts). As far as I'm concerned this was (and still is) the hardest rule to get used to. It simply doesn't make sense to me, and it always feels like an accident waiting to happen.

- Cars over 4 years old need to go to the car doctor to have a check up. This is done every 2 years. Once you get the all clear you'll get a piece of paper and you're right to go for another 2 years.

- As crazy as this may sound, try and stick to the speed limits even though nobody else does. Rules are 130 Km/h on motorways and generally 100 Km/h when it rains/snows. Regional roads; 90 Km/h. Built-up areas (villages and towns) 50 Km/h. Low visibility less than 50 meters, 50 Km/h.

- Speed Cameras are alive and well. However, everybody knows exactly where the cameras are located. One just needs to check the Internet to discover their precise location; consequently, one simply slows down on approach before speeding up again. That being the case, I wonder why they bother putting them up in the first place? In Australia they hide the cameras, and frequently move them around to keep you guessing. They also have people with high tech speed-reading equipment lurking behind bushes. In that sense, the French are way behind the revenue raising ballgame, which surprises me. Mind you if the traffic police started lurking behind bushes in France there'd be a national strike to settle the 'injustice' of it all.

Tips:
- People coming from the right have priority.

- If in doubt get into the slow lane or get abused.
- French people are questionable drivers (so don't take any abuse personal).
- Don't buy a car in France; instead, buy in Germany, England, Belgium as it is cheaper to buy there. There will be a bit of paper work involved, but that's France for you.

No sugar-coating here - the French drive like there is no tomorrow.

I don't know if it's because they drink too much (Dutch courage), or whatever else the reason. To be sure, there are strict drink-driving rules in place, but nobody ever seems to get breathalyzed. In Australia if you get caught driving after 2 glasses of wine, they'll lock you up and throw away the key, whereas here they're just as likely to ask you about the vintage. Just to clarify, I'm talking about the south. In the north they are a lot stricter.

On a positive note, driving here can be an absolute pleasure when you're ambling along French country roads (preferably with a non-French person driving), embarking on a magical mystery tour of winding roads, Médoc vineyards and medieval castles perched on top of historic villages.

Having said that, just make sure to hurry things along. Be quick to take in the view, take the photo and buy the T-shirt before somebody cuts you off by tooting their horn and hollering obscenities such as "Connard!" "Con!" or "Va Te Faire Foutre!" Translations unnecessary. This is a clean book.

In Case of Emergency dial:

15 - For an ambulance

18 - If there's a fire

17 - To notify the police of drunken driving and/or road blockages

Working in France

"Choose a job you love, and you will never have to work a day in your life."

(Confucius)

Earning a Living

The best advice I can give you is this: If you want to be location independent try a multi-faceted approach by learning trades and skills that can be applied anywhere in the world.

Going the conventional route, as in finding a regular job is not easy but it can be done. Here's how:

- Do your research before you leave home (what's the demand in your area of expertise?).
- Be prepared to change course and drop all your perceived ideas about who you are and what you want to do because something completely different may present itself.

- Take every opportunity to meet people.

- Make learning the language your priority (don't do what I did for the first year or so and become a recluse). Think about it: why would anyone want to give you a job if you can't speak the language?

- If your French is basic and you think there's probably no hope for you, consider teaching English, although speaking some French would still be a huge bonus.

Where to look:

- Scan **The Connexion**, http://www.connexionfrance.com/, an English language newspaper in France for jobs.
- **Join forums**. I found lots of valuable information on http://www.expatforum.com/
- Look at **ANPE** http://www.pole-emploi.fr/accueil/, the French job center or Adecco, http://www.adecco.fr/Pages/default.aspx, which offers temporary work.
- **Keljob** http://www.keljob.com/ (search engine for all sorts of jobs)
- **Jobpilot** http://www.jobpilot.fr/ (as above)
- **English Speaking Jobs in France**, https://www.thelocal.fr/jobs/
- Check out **Craigslist** – great site for jobs and pretty much anything else for pretty much every city around the world, eg. http://www.paris.en.craigslist.fr/
- Alternatively you could place an ad in French Newspapers like **Le Monde** http://www.lemonde.fr or **Le Figaro** http://www.lefigaro.fr/
- **Create a website or blog** and publish your CV
- Join and build a profile on **LinkedIn** http://www.linkedin.com
- Join an outsourcing site like **upwork**, https://www.upwork.com/
- (I use this from time to time). All you need to do is create a profile, and post it on the site. The basic service is free. Once you get a job they simply take a small commission. You can open a **paypal** account to get paid. Or else choose wire-transfers or direct deposit.
- **Get involved in the community** and you'll more than likely find something. Word of mouth, that's how things work around here.

Tip: Did you know that France has an agreement with the U.S. that provides Social Security advantages for people who have worked in both countries? More info here:

http://www.ssa.gov/international/Agreement_Pamphlets/france.html

Creative ways to make a living

(without the traditional 'job')

If you don't find a regular job, and/or don't want to, why not create your own? Don't believe the hype about needing a job. What you need is work, not necessarily a contract to slavery. Instead, why not work for yourself? Do work you enjoy. Do work that you do well, that you love, that's part of who you are.

The following information is for the kind of person who values life and quality time over bundles of money.

Ideas for starting a micro-business:

Consulting - Anything that fits into this category can be done online, via the phone and/or Skype.

Teaching – an oldie but a goodie. If you like teaching but don't like having to stand in front of a class I have good news for you. These days you can teach anything from English as a second language to Yoga, online via Skype. All you need is a laptop and reliable Internet connection. If, however you enjoy the personal interaction when teaching, there are various options to choose from: Adult schools, Private one-on-one tuition; private schools for children and teaching agencies like…

Acadomia http://www.acadomia.fr/

Capcours http://www.capcours.com/

Wall Street English http://www.wallstreetinstitute.fr/

In most cases a TEFL or CELTA qualification helps, although it is not always required. A knowledge of Business English is even more useful because a lot of companies in France pay for up to 20 hours of employee training per year, which provides a lot of business for the agencies and international schools. On average, teaching jobs pay around €15 per hour net.

Gardening (think new trends like helping people set up their own vegetable patch in the growing economic decline). These days a lot of people have the desire but not necessarily the know-how.

Cleaning/Housekeeping - Think aging population. Most elderly people want to keep their independence but need help in order to do so.

Babysitting – if you like kids, why not run a local crèche?

Handy man - if you have manual skills you're in luck. After that it's word of mouth.

Renovations - (as above)

Building - (as above)

Massage

Yoga/Meditation teaching – why not create your own home studio?

The Healing Arts

Filmmaking - Nowadays you can shoot a no-budget film and publish it online. Great news for filmmakers! No need to beg for money and wait years to create your film. The Internet makes it all possible by eliminating the fat middlemen. Below, an example of someone who did just that. He created a no-budget film and put it on the Internet. The film went viral. He then started charging people a small fee to download it, earning the guy €200 000 within a few months:

http://www.filmmakermagazine.com/news/2011/07/polish-brothers-release-successful-no-budget-movie-on-itunes/

Fruit picking - seasonal work only, but who wants to work all year long?

Editing and proofreading books and papers (my bread and butter - feel free to drop me a line if you need a good editor/proofreader)

Be a tour-guide - think outside the square. Shopping tours, painting tours, cooking tours, local food specialty tours, special nooks and crannies tours etc.

Start a Bed and Breakfast - not a new concept but again think small. For example you could buy a run-down barn with an extra room or two. Create a website and advertise on the Internet. Keep it simple.

Writing – write travel articles, start a blog, write ebooks.

Some helpful websites for freelance travel writers:

http://www.eurotrip.com/

http://www.presstrips.com/

http://www.freelancetravelwriter.com/

http://www.travelintelligence.com/

Here's a link to a travel writing course:

http://matadoru.com/travel-courses/travel-writing/

Translation

Interpreting

Web design

Illustration

What about your current job? When you think about it, these days a lot of jobs can be done from home. Be it travel agent work, real estate, consulting, therapy, accounting, it's endless. Does your current job allow location independence?

Make art, jewelry and clothing etc and sell it in your 'virtual' shop.

Etsy http://www.etsy.com is a huge market place where artists can sell their pieces online, anything from hand made to vintage items. You get to cash in on your passion and the buyer gets an original, well-priced piece. Win-win. Another bonus - no overheads. I love shopping via Etsy because I know I'm supporting artists and people who like to do things on their own terms.

Photography - check out online sites like istockphoto and shutterpoint
http://www.istockphoto.com/

http://www.shutterpoint.com, which let you sell your prints online, and/or why not sell your prints via your blog or etsy?

Be an Auto-Entrepreneur – pay low taxes

In France, as an auto-entrepreneur or person who runs a small micro-business, you'll be placed in a lower tax category. Surprisingly, registering as an auto-entrepreneur is pretty easy. Here's the official site: Portail Officiel des Auto-Entrepreneurs. http://www.lautoentrepreneur.fr/. You can sign up online. If you happen to have a "real job" on the side, along with your business there's no problem with having both.

So why worry about taxes? If you're not making a fortune they'll be relatively small. Depends on how you look at things. You may not be a millionaire but who cares when you're living the lifestyle of one.

Don't think in terms of numbers; think in terms of quality of life. Time is everything and you'll no longer be busy squandering away your one and only precious life.

Remember to stay open to what emerges. You have a new slate, a carte blanche and nobody knows you on the other side of the world. What a perfect time (to not necessarily reinvent yourself) but to be the person you were always meant to be.

For extra inspiration, check out **zenhabits**

http://zenhabits.net/the-get-started-now-guide-to-becoming-self-employed/ where you'll find a massive amount of information on how to become self-employed (and more) without the necessary headaches that come with the territory when we think in terms of business and dollars.

Working online

The Internet has opened doors for creatives and non-creatives alike. All sorts of options and opportunities not previously available are suddenly up for grabs, which is why The Web is becoming more prominent, especially in the lives of expats, making autonomy not only possible but also easy.

Nowadays there is a fast emerging new breed of people/adventurers who've decided not to settle for mediocrity. Location independent folk known as 'digital nomads'. All YOU need for that to happen is to offer a valuable service or information online and you can work from anywhere. Cool? Cool.

Another plus about working online is that it opens up your market, literally placing the entire world at your fingertips. Think about it. Working online means you are not limited to working for a French company, and/or obligated to speak French. One thing is certain. Once you start working for yourself (albeit at a pittance compared to what you're used to), there's no going back.

"I'm a slow walker, but I never walk back."

(Abraham Lincoln)

Although the micro-Internet business concept is still in its infancy, it won't be long before more people see the advantage of working this way. If you already work online then it's really a no brainer. Who cares where you do it – as long as you have a phone (better still, use Skype, http://www.skype.com, which is free) and a reliable Internet connection.

If, however, you like to dream a little bigger there are still plenty of opportunities for entrepreneurs in the good old staple areas of real estate, hospitality, and import/export.

Art For Art's Sake

"As an artist, a man has no home in Europe save in Paris"

(Friedrich Nietzsche)

In Australia, whenever people asked me what I did for a living, I hardly ever told them I was an actor. Instead I used to talk about my 'day job'.

Back home, if you tell people you're an actor, usually they nod sympathetically and the conversation stops there. Why? It is not considered a real job, a serious profession or worse, it is ridiculed and broken down to the lowest common denominator.

"What TV shows have you been on?"

As if that's a sort of measurement of your worth as an actor. Problem is that TV (in Australia) is the last thing any real actor wants to do as it's about as far from art as you can get.

Even so, you have to eat, right?

When I graduated from acting school my teachers told me to bypass Australia and go straight to Europe. Some of my peers where told to head to the US. I don't have the 'Hollywood look' and/or desire to carve up my face and body in order to obtain it, so I never even gave the US as second's thought.

Europe made sense. After all, it's where I was born. Still, I didn't listen. Instead, I stayed in Australia and became a person who had to work shitty jobs in order to maintain an almost non-existent acting career. Twelve years later I'm finally in Europe but I have to wonder whether or not it's all a little too late.

Long story short, my life as an actor became a stepping-stone to writing. And though I stand to be judged in terms of my work as a writer, at least I don't have to wait for a nod from certain 'producers' to give me permission to do my work. There is nothing and nobody to stop me from writing. Nothing and nobody to stop me from hitting the publish button. And yes, there is a point to this tale.

"Sometimes the only way you can win is to stay out of the game."

(Ashley Brilliant)

Point is, the Internet has changed the rules of the game, leveled the playing field and opened previously closed doors for all types of artists. There's never been a better time to deconstruct, break down and reinvent the notion of barriers, borders and foreign languages.

For example, I look forward to one day being able to write in French. When you write in another language you make mistakes. And sometimes those mistakes turn out to be gold because you are most likely expressing yourself in a way that perhaps a French person would not.

Recently I saw a documentary about an American writer in Germany. She spoke German and wrote in German but because she was not a native German speaker she wasn't able to express herself in the way a native German writer could. Nonetheless, it didn't stop her from writing. Uberhaupt nicht! Au contraire! She found success in spite of herself.

When you break the rules, that's when real art happens. Just as when you drop a line or screw up on stage, real (as opposed to contrived) theater happens.

If you're an artist reading this you already know the arts are a highly respected medium in France, and an artist is never questioned, hassled, ridiculed or asked whether or not he/she will ever get a real job.

One is also never asked to reel off any shows one has performed in - in order to somehow prove one's validity. Neither, it seems are actors measured simply by their looks. And yes, France does have her fair share of beautiful (as well as left-off-center) people in the entertainment industry, but at least they can act. If they can't, they don't last. Isn't that refreshing?

What's more, in France, physical age is no barrier in terms of continuing one's career. Quite the opposite. Here, a little maturity makes the actors more interesting - adding depth to their performance. And yes, believe it or not, a well-weathered face is even considered sexy.

In Australia, when an actress or (female) newsreader reaches a certain age, she is slowly phased out and replaced by a younger version. Mature 'working' actors do exist, but they are few and far between.

If, for example, an Australian actress wants to work in the US, she is generally discouraged to try unless she is in her early twenties. I've even heard stories of young Australian actresses being persuaded (by Australian producers) to conform and preserve their faces with regular Botox injections - at the tender age of 23. Some don't but most do, for fear of losing their place in the sun.

How sad that we revere the notion of physical perfection above talent. After all, the art of story telling and translating human emotions doesn't stop at a certain age. Seemingly, that doesn't matter in the mainstream world of cinema where evidently all one needs to make a film is a superhero running to escape whatever special effect is blowing up behind him, some 'eye-candy' actress running along beside him and lots of ammunition.

In Europe, the 'Blockbuster' formula is far less prevalent, if at all. Thank goodness, to this day, the European audience prefers stories about humanity. Simple tales about ordinary people. People of all ages, shapes, sizes and color.

But I digress. Here's what happened to me:

A few months ago I went to check out my options for work with **pole-emploi** - http://www.pole-emploi.fr/accueil/ - a local government agency that helps people find work.

If you're in between jobs, you can register for a minimum payment from the **Caisse D'allocations Familiales** (CAF), - the whole deal works hand in hand with pole emploi. CAF is not a Social Security or unemployment benefit, as we know it. It's more like a payment from the government to keep you from starving while you continue to look for work. You can get more information about the CAF by checking out their website: http://www.caf.fr

So, after a brief interview during which I handed in a CV consisting of acting work I had done, I was given a list of the following:

- A comprehensive guide for all directeurs de casting in Marseille.

- A list of anybody involved in the arts.
- A website whereby I could create an acting profile.
- €400 per month from (CAF) to tied me over until I find a job.

Having created the required online work profile, any possible job matches are sent straight to my inbox. Recently I sent 20 introductory emails to local casting agents - 3 of which responded, so stay tuned...

Plainly from my point of view, it feels good to be in a country that values and appreciates culture. If you are involved in the arts in any way, shape or form, you know what I mean.

Note: Throughout the entire experience, I was never asked about a 'backup'. In their eyes I'm an actor and that seems to be enough (no cheesy 'day job' occupations required). Come to think of it, I haven't yet told them I'm also a writer. Better to ease them in gently, *non*?

> "In America only the successful writer is important, in France all writers are important, in England no writer is important, and in Australia you have to explain what a writer is."
>
> (Geoffrey Cottrell)

Artist Resources

When you're the new kid in town you need to find your tribe…

For Film makers and Actors

Film Acting Paris (short film making course for actors, directors writers and composers)

http://www.filmactingparis.com/summer_workshop.php?lang=en

Bilingual Acting Workshop

http://www.bilingualacting.com/

Acting International (Bilingual Theatre and Cinema School)

http://www.acting-international.com/

Agent - Voyez Mon Agent

(Agency representing artists in music, cinema, theatre and television)

http://www.vma.fr/

UBBA (artist agency representing actors, writers, directors and composers)

http://www.ubba.eu/

Artmedia

(The first European artistic agency, representing 600 artists - including some major stars - of all fields) http://www.artmedia.fr/agence.cfm

Casting Agencies (listed in alphabetical order)

http://www.agencesartistiques.com/liste.cfm?rbrq=agences

Agents (Full list in alphabetical order)

http://www.agencesartistiques.com/liste.cfm?rbrq=agents

Conservatoire National Superieur d'Art Dramatique (Paris) - If you're serious, about acting, this one's the top acting school in France.

http://www.cnsad.fr/1.aspx

Uni France Films (Website Promoting French Cinema)

http://en.unifrance.org/

Cannes Film Festival (official website)

http://www.festival-cannes.com/

French Cinema and TV website

http://www.lefilmfrancais.com/

La Replique (Marseille) -A professional actors' collective organization

http://www.lareplique.org/

Best movie theatres in Paris

https://www.localers.com/travel-guide/paris/our-picks-paris/the-best-movie-theatres-in-paris

For Writers

Paris Writers Retreat (professional intensives)

http://www.pariswritersretreat.com/

Secrets of Paris (links for writers pursuing a writing career in Europe)

http://www.secretsofparis.com/writers-france/

English Language Bookshops

Shakespeare and Company (Paris) – This famous Parisian institution is a one-stop bookstore and resource center for writers and readers. Here, you'll find information on workshops, festivals, jobs, writing classes and other events.

http://www.shakespeareandcompany.com/

The Abbey Bookshop (Paris)

https://abbeybookshop.wordpress.com/about/

Tea and Tattered Pages (Paris) is a second hand bookstore and tea room in Paris.

https://bonjourparis.com/archives/paris-used-bookstores-tea-and-tattered-pages/

English Bookstores in France

https://www.wanderingeducators.com/best/traveling/20-best-english-bookstores-paris.html

Maurel – English Bookshop (Marseille)

http://www.librairie-internationale-maurel.com/index.htm

Painting

Ecole de Beaux Art de Paris (School of Fine Arts) This one's the tip of the top.
http://www.ensba.fr/

Study Art in France (Links to courses throughout France in film, painting, languages and more)
http://www.studyabroadlinks.com/search/France/Study_Art/index.html

Visual Arts

Vingt Paris Magazine – "comprehensive hub for visual arts information and resources in Paris"
http://www.vingtparismagazine.com/

Music and Dance

Conservatoire de Paris – College of music and dance
http://www.cnsmdp.fr/

School of Dance
http://dance.fsu.edu/programs-2/fsu-dance-in-paris/

Opening a Bank Account in France

Whether you're moving permanently or simply buying a holiday shack, you're better off having a French bank account (easier for paying your mortgage and/or bills). Also you can set up a direct debit a 'prelevement' (paid every 3 months).

Documents needed to open a French Bank Account:

- 2 forms of ID
- Proof of your address in France
- A recent credit card statement (if you are a non-resident)
- References from your bank at home

- Birth certificate

You will then receive:

- A carte bleue, which is a combination of a debit/ATM card and also functions as a credit card outside France.
- A pin number for cash withdrawals and over the counter payments. (In France you can pay for almost anything with the carte bleue).
- A chequebook with your RIBs (slips of paper with all your account details). Although cheques are old hat in other parts of the world, the French still use them. Dinosaur system I know, but here, cheques can come in handy, especially in rural areas.
- Online banking – also used frequently as everything is becoming more automated.

A friendly word of warning!

Once you've opened your account, make sure you make regular deposits and withdrawals otherwise the following might happen to you…

Due to the massive overseas ATM withdrawal fees, I decided to open an account with HSBC in Marseille in order to transfer funds from my HSBC Australia account. I then went on holidays for 3 months. When I got back I was surprised to find the bank had decided to close my account due to 'lack of movement'. Luckily the money was still there. I withdrew it and that was that. They then asked if I wanted to re-open the account. No thanks, I told them. Once was more than enough. This would never happen in Australia! Imagine a bank deciding what to do with your account?!

List of Major French banks

Caisse d'Epargne (I use this bank for no reason other than my husband has an account with them (meaning they are obviously flexible and tolerant with people's 'movements' or lack thereof).

Credit Agricole

Credit du Nord

La Banque Postale

Barclays France (English website)

BNP Paribas

CIC

Société Générale

ING Direct

HCBC (Grrr…)

Credit Lyonnais

Britline

Credit Mutuel

MonaBanq

Note: Banks generally stay open between 9-12pm and close for lunch until 2-2.30pm, then re-open until 7pm Tuesdays to Fridays. They're usually closed on Mondays and Sundays. Nobody likes Mondays, least of all the French.

Tips:

Ask your bank about your options in transferring your account to another bank/branch in France. This could work out a lot easier than opening a new account in France.

If you want to keep your bank account at home make sure to give them your new address. Sometimes banks don't forward cards/credit cards etc via mail, so you may have to make special arrangements.

Before you leave home, don't forget to tell your bank you're heading overseas so they can 'unlock' your credit card for international use. This (sometimes) happens for your own protection, but when it does it can be highly inconvenient.

French Taxes

True, France has a rather naughty reputation for outrageously high taxes. That being so, one can't help but wonder why the French capitulate on this one? When more often than not, it seems, the thrill of the 1968 revolutionary fervor is permanently ingrained in their spirit. Supposedly, since then, they've never stopped protesting and every time they have an occasion to take it to the streets, they will.

Could the French tax system, then, present a seeming disparity in the nations' psyche? Not likely, and here are a couple of reasons as to why the French don't bother to put up a fight:

They get to go to a doctor when they are sick (as already mentioned, 84 percent of the French are satisfied with their system of health care).

Their kids get to have an education without having to pay for college fees (as in pay them back for the rest of their lives).

Goes without saying that the French tax system is way too dense a subject for me to tackle (kind of like a can of worms) and I am certainly no expert in these matters. Hence, if you are after some information on French taxation (in English), you will find a straightforward, simplified version here: http://www.riviera.angloinfo.com/countries/france/intax.asp.

For a more detailed version (also in English), head for the French tax authorities. Keep in mind that some of the information is probably dated (things like rates), nonetheless if you want the right information straight from the horses mouth it's all here:

http://www.impots.gouv.fr/portal/deploiement/p1/fichedescriptive_1006/fichedescriptive_1006.pdf

If you prefer to read a highly recommended book (via forums), check out "Taxation in France" – a foreign Perspective, written by Virginie Deflassieux.

http://www.amazon.fr/Taxation-France-2008-Foreign-Perspective/dp/0954349040

The book is written from a non-French person point of view for anyone considering investing in France and it covers the following topics:

- The French tax system
- Advice on retiring
- Guide to income tax
- Wealth tax
- Corporation tax
- Capital gains tax
- Explanation of terms used and information about residence issues

If you're anything like me and not particularly interested in governmental literature and/or taxes, see below for a basic income bracket and tax guideline (based on rates prior to deductions you may be entitled to).

Calculation of income tax: 2011 rates:

For earnings up to 5 963 euros: 0

5964 euros - 11 896 euros: 5.50 percent

11 897 euros - 26 420 euros: 14 percent

26 421 euros - 70 839 euros: 30 percent

In excess of 70 830 euros: 41percent

As I said, I'm no authority on the subject, but this is how I see things:

If you have no overheads, debts or major bills, you don't need all that much money.

Less income = less taxes

Less taxes = less stress

Less stress = more living, and more freedom.

Moving your Pet to France

Fortunately there's no need to say goodbye to your furry friends when you move to France. France is pet friendly (almost to a fault) and won't treat your little buddy as if it's a public health threat. You can bring up to five dogs and/or cats to France (as long as the animals are at least 3 months old). You can also bring birds, rodents, amphibians and snakes.

To do list:

- You'll need an EU Pet Passport: http://www.pettravel.com/immigration/France.cfm
- Get your pet microchip-ed or tattooed to EU norms or bring a reader that will read your chip
- A valid rabies vaccination certificate (dated at least 30 days before the move but no older than a year)
- A letter from your vet stating your pet is in good health (letter must not be more than 4 months old)
- When everything's done, you'll need to get all the paperwork stamped by a USDA certified Veterinarian before you can board the plane

Some useful pet websites:

(For a more detailed and constantly up to date info on moving your pet to France).

http://franceintheus.org/spip.php?article783

http://www.veterinaire.fr

http://www.chien.com

http://www.animal-services.com

http://www.wanimo.com

France - Warts And All

"Every 60 seconds you spend upset is one minute of happiness you'll never get back."

(Web Wisdom)

The French & Rudeness

Recently, the ministry of tourism launched a new campaign with the intention of making France and the French are tad more welcoming. True.

In France there are rude people and polite people like everywhere else, (though France should not to be confused with Paris, which regularly treats everyone with disdain, tourists or French alike).

Generally speaking, the French often appear to be rude for a couple of reasons:

- The don't smile if they don't want to
- Their body and facial language is entirely unique to their culture
- They don't do anything they don't want to do
- They say 'no' if they disagree
- They don't do 'false niceties'

Simply put, they are not so much rude as straightforward. And proud to be so. Moreover, I'm sure half the time they don't even realize they are coming across in a negative way because quite frankly they don't waste precious time and energy analyzing whether or not they are. Neither do they split hairs over second guessing people and seeking approval.

Think about it. The Gallic Rooster, one of the emblems of France, is a domestic, male fowl that lives in its own shit. Even so, with shit incessantly clinging to its feet, it sings proudly. Shit or no shit, life goes on as it continues to sing out of tune, protest loudly and mate frequently.

When you walk into a shop in Australia or some other parts of the world, it is normal practice for the sales assistant to acknowledge you and make friendly chit chat.

"Hello, how's your day going?" they'll holler across the room with a beaming fake smile.

We all know their concern for our wellbeing is not genuine, yet we expect to be asked nonetheless. The French don't do this. They don't ask. This is why people feel as though they're being ignored. To be sure they are, but not intentionally so.

Last but not least, try not to over-generalize. People in the north are different to the southerners. Parisians are different to the French. Not all French are Parisian and not all Parisians are French. End of story.

Navigating The Dog Merde

The French love their dogs, and their pooches are allowed anywhere. Restaurants, cafés, shops, public transport, public buildings. They're also allowed to 'go' almost anywhere. Not strictly speaking but let's face it, they do. Hence, it's always best to engage your peripheral vision when walking around the streets. Stepping in dog shit is part and parcel of your integration, and you will not feel 'as one' with the place until you do. When you do step in the dog merde, all you can do is hope it was with your left foot, which apparently guarantees good luck. The possible ramifications of 'right foot' stomping are usually not discussed.

Public Toilets

You know those little tissue packs your mother used to hand you before you walked out the door? Consider them good training because in France you should never leave home without them. It's the least you can do. Unfortunately those all-in-one plastic suits, plastic gloves and disinfectants don't come in small enough packs or else we'd all use them (another million dollar idea!). Fact is with French toilets you never know what you're gonna get. And no, it ain't nothing like a box of chocolates. On occasion, be prepared to be pleasantly surprised, but more often than not, just be prepared.

French Drivers (see also 'Driving in France' chapter)

Inevitably, the only time my husband and I argue we're in the car. Not sure how or why this happens, but it's almost like living with a Dr Jekyll and Mr Hyde. As soon as he gets behind the wheel, he's weaving in and out of traffic at death defying speed, verbally insulting anybody driving at (or slightly below) the legal speed limit and growling at any unsuspecting person sitting at a red light for a micro-second too long. Thus, whenever in a car, I cease to recognize the person I am married to.

Survival Tactics :

- Anticipate when the light is about to change to green before it actually does. If you start driving when the light changes to green (as would be expected in every other normal country) you will be abused by blaring car horns, verbal insults and wild manic stares from the person behind or next to you. Why? Because you didn't slam your foot on the accelerator the millisecond before the lights changed.
- When you get a fine it is an automatic permission slip to insult the police/parking inspector. You are in your right to do so. In fact, it is almost expected. If in doubt, remember the French motto liberté, égalité, fraternité. Also, it helps to be a female in this situation. Just saying.
- Watch out for 'scooter people' driving on the footpath (usually in the opposite direction). If you happen to be on the footpath at the same time and you value your life, get out of the way.

Parking

Since living in France I have discovered what bumper bars are all about. The French park wherever they want. Where there's a half spot they'll squeeze in and cars literally get bumped out of the way to make room. Sidewalks, double-parking, no-standing zones, towing-zones, nothing's off limits. These days more people are choosing the tiny 'smart cars' because they are easier to 'badly-park'. You can park them vertically or horizontally.

Smoking

You might as well take up the habit. Although smoking is now forbidden *inside* restaurants, bars, café's and (some) public places there is no way you'll be able to *not* passive smoke anywhere else.

If you're sitting outside at a café terrace for example, no amount of tut-tutting, shaking your head or shifting in your chair will make any difference whatsoever. Once you are outdoors it's anyone's game. Occasionally indoors too. In certain corner bars or Tabacs smokers still light 'em up and suck 'em down. Nobody bats an eye. It's not exactly allowed, but the French are not exactly worried about breaking a tiny law here and there. Fact is people don't get their knickers in knot about it here as much as some other parts of the world. Here, the smokers outnumber. They win.

To illustrate: Recently, Yann Barthès, a killer TV journalist from channel Canal+ interviewed the famous French film actress Catherine Deneuve, during which they both lit up on National TV. Illegal? Yes. Did they care? I think not.

Most probably, you know all this already and to be perfectly blunt, if you don't like smoking and/or smokers and/or being within a 1 meter radius of the 'filthy habit', maybe it's best to reconsider your options. Either stay where you are or move to Bhutan, the world's first non-smoking nation where it is illegal to smoke in public or to sell tobacco.

The French Timetable

I'm almost tempted to write the shortest paragraph in history…

"There isn't one."

I'll try, however, and extrapolate just a little. Most shops (except department stores) close for long lunch breaks and typically reopen by 2.30 or 3pm. Restaurants close in the afternoon. A lot of places are shut on Mondays and Sundays (I'm guessing they've simply taken the 'nobody likes Monday's' mood to the next level).

Another wacky timetable example - when the majority of French people start work after the summer vacation in August/September, a lot of them start back on a Friday (depending on the number of days in any given year). I suppose starting back on Fridays makes French sense as it eases grumpy post-holiday people in gently. Not a bad concept and *tres* civilized, I think you'll agree.

Just like everything else here, the local timetable (code word for 'let's work the least amount possible'), takes a while to get the hang of and there's no point in fighting 'what is'. All you can do is take a load off, chill and go with the flow.

French Bureaucracy

Yes the thing about this part is that it's the most annoying and at the same time the most important when it comes to living here legally. I'm afraid there is no back door escape. Even when you think you've hit a home run, got your visa, and handed over all your intimate data (including what your great grandmother ate for breakfast) there's more.

The main problem with French Bureaucracy is this: when it comes to government matters, the left hand has no idea what the right hand is scratching, and that about sums it up.

On the level. Sometimes I wish I'd never done any of this officially. If I had the opportunity to do it all again, I'd buy a sailboat and become a perpetual traveler (stay tuned for an update on this thought). http://www.lifehack.org/articles/lifestyle/would-you-be-a-perpetual-traveler-or-a-world-citizen.html

As things stand, I'm half way through the 'branding of the cow' process and may as well continue.

Tip: Smile, breathe and go slowly.

Checklist for Documents Needed

Before you come to France, you're best to collect all your documents and stick them in a file (preferably a sturdy one as you'll be using it a lot).

Here's a list of the most common documents required:

- Valid Passport
- Visa and/or work permit (if applicable)
- Your driving license, vehicle insurance certificates and registration documents (must be presented at controls)
- Birth certificate
- Marriage papers/ divorce papers
- Livret de famille – a document you receive when you get married in France and/or to a French person. Basically it's a booklet in which they record the names of your children, parents in law etc.
- Proof of health insurance or a European health card (if applicable)
- Sworn translated copies of your birth certificate, marriage certificate and all your diplomas (better to get them translated in France by a registered local translator. Ask for a list at your local town hall)
- Last 3 payslips
- Last 3 rent slips (if applicable)
- Proof of ownership of a property and/or proof of residence
- A couple of utility bills no older than 6 months
- Full bank details of your bank in your current place of residence
- Proof of financial resources (statements, reference letter from your bank)
- New Employment contract (if applicable)
- Updated version of your CV, cover letters and references translated into French (best to have paper as well as electronic formats of these)
- Colored 6-12 passport size photographs (optional as you can get those in the photo booths all over France)
- Tax records
- A police clearance certificate (just in case)
- Medical certificates and records (also dental)

Note: Make 3-4 copies of everything and keep it in a file. Take the entire file with you to any and every appointment in France. That includes carte de séjour renewals and/or appointments for a filling at the dentist. (You never know what they'll ask for on the day, so be prepared, be armed, be patient and I promise, you will conquer that bureaucracy beast!)

More Resources

General information about living in France

http://www.americansinfrance.net

https://www.angloinfo.com/france

http://www.frenchentree.com/

http://www.francethisway.com/

http://www.francetoday.com/

Check the following sites for Expats Clubs and Associations

Just Landed

https://www.justlanded.com/english/France

http://www.expatica.com/fr/

Expat Focus

http://www.expatfocus.com/expatriate-france-groups

https://www.thelocal.fr/20141114/the-best-anglo-clubs-in-france

Expat Cricket in France

http://www.french-property.com/news/french_life/expat_cricket_france/

Expat Exchange

http://www.expatexchange.com/rspnet.cfm?networkID=45&rid=74

American Expat in France

http://www.americanexpatinfrance.com/2011/06/25/american-clubs-of-france-newsletter-events-in-france/

Expatforum (information about Football clubs in France)

http://www.expatforum.com/expats/france-expat-forum-expats-living-france/92038-football-clubs-france.html

Paris Voice "A webzine for English Speaking Parisians"

http://www.parisvoice.com/

Good (fun) Books about life in France

A year in Provence and *Hotel Pastis* by Peter Mayle

Anything by Stephen Clark - *A year in the Merde; Merde Actually; Merde Happens; Dial M for Merde; Talk to the Snail; 1000 Years of Annoying the French; Paris Revealed – The Secret Life of a City* (Can you tell I'm a huge fan?)

The Olive Farm by Carol Drinkwater

French or Foe and *Love a la Francaise* by Polly Platt

Chocolat by Joanne Harris (also a movie starring Juliette Binoche)

Petite Anglaise: In Paris, in love, in trouble by Catherine Sanderson

Almost French: A new life in Paris by Sarah Turnbull (love this one)

Two Lipsticks and a Lover by Helena Frith Powell

Entre Nous: A woman's guide to finding her inner French girl and *What French Women know about love, sex and other matters of the heart and mind* by Debra Ollivier

Culture Shock! France: A Guide to Customs and Etiquette by Sally Adamson Taylor

Living and Working in France by David Hampshire

French Women don't sleep alone by Jamie Cat Callan

French Men on Love & Women by Tanja Bulatovic (Shameless self-plug ! :) …

https://www.amazon.com/French-Love-Women-Tanja-Bulatovic-ebook/dp/B01M184PUI

Emergency Phone Numbers

Medical Assistance – Samu (15)

Police – (17)

Fire Brigade – Pompiers – (18)

European Emergency Call – (112)

Homeless – (115)

Child Abuse – (119)

Alcohol Abuse/ Alcoholics Anonymous (33) 01 46 34 59 65

SOS Help is a listening service for English speakers in France (available every day between 3-11pm) 01 46 21 46 46

Chapter 3

Food, Love and Wine
(not necessarily in that order)

"I'd like to French pastry myself to death, right now."
(Manhattan Murder Mystery - 1993 film)

Tasty plump oysters. Fresh black truffles. The best artichokes you'll ever taste. Fat coeur de boeuf tomatoes. Delicious breads. Fava beans (the kind Hannibal Lecter liked), and yes; lest not forget the 400-plus varieties of melt-in-your-mouth cheese!

When you look a little closer, the food in France is part of the whole picture of seduction. And here, romance is easy. Even if you're hurting like most people from la crise économique, pretty much anyone can afford to grab a bottle of wine and some cheese for an impromptu picnic.

In my past life, eating breakfast, lunch or dinner was simply a means to an end. Since moving to France, however, I have developed a new relationship to food. Nowadays, each meal is an event. A special moment to savor along with the meal.

In a way, too, the process of French-style hunter gathering, preparing, and tasting has become an emotional lifeline for me - a reason to go out and mix with the crowd. Cooking provided a creative outlet - something to do with my hands when I couldn't speak French with our dinner guests. Food as nurturer, healer, comforter and teacher.

In spite of the fact that I'm no connoisseur or brilliant cook, I've become somewhat fussy. Even on a low budget, fresh ingredients and home cooking have moved to the top of my list of priorities.

From buttery, warm croissants & coffee in the morning to the ritual of fresh produce shopping, all day lunches and gorgeous picnics - to taking photos of the food I eat and the meals Fabrice creates from scratch.

All in all, the France & food message is this:

- Celebrate life
- Honor the self
- Indulge in the time it takes to do so

The French love their food passionately, no secrets there. It must be said however, that there's no such thing as one category of 'French food'. Although there are the trusty staples like bread, cheese, and pâté, the country's regional dishes vary intensely. You won't find the same specialties in Nantes that you will find in Marseille for example.

But it's not only about the food; it's about socializing, the ritual, which involves enjoying the company of friends and family. Simple gatherings around a table, which anchor and energize like nothing else can.

At work too, it's about heading out to a restaurant or café to eat a proper meal at lunchtime instead of staying at the office in front of the computer screen. More often than not the French receive a dejeuner coupon from their respective employers to go and eat a free lunch. All in all, it goes to show how much the French actually value fine quality.

Good food is highly affordable. The cost of food and drinks in France is considerably lower compared to other European nations. Why? Because the French grow most of their own stuff and are one of the world's largest exporters of wine, beer, cider, bread, pastries and wheat products (see 'cost of living' chapter).

As an aside: This is strictly between you and me... don't tell the French but truth be told, French taste buds where somewhat crude in early times and it was (according to a food historian by the name of Waverly Root), the Romans' knowledge which heavily influenced what is today known as French Cuisine.

Food Laws and Rituals

In relation to food, there are a few strange practices I'd like to illuminate here. For one, expect to witness obsessive discussions about culinary details. For instance, when at the table, be prepared to talk about the intricacies of a good quality haricot *vert* bean for the entire duration of the meal. For the haricot novice, this may present a challenge in terms of contributing to the conversation.

For one, your mouth will be full as you nod in agreement; for another, what can one possibly contribute? You've probably never given the humble bean a single moments thought in your life and/or probably you're thinking…

"Who gives a toss... it's a bean for Christ's sake!"

But not for long. Soon, you too will sway and succumb to the culinary temptations, conversations, rituals and laws, which are not only there to seduce you but to offer a new way of life. Soon, you too will not only be able to discuss the (not-so-humble) string bean in great detail, you will want to. And when you do, want to, that is, you will know that you have finally arrived.

Shouting matches/arguments at lunch or dinners are in fact just passionate conversations. Indeed it can feel as though one is witnessing a long-standing family-feud-nightmare where in fact one is most likely witnessing an explosive discussion about politics, religion or sex.

Tip: If you get caught in this situation, don't fret and don't wonder. It's all perfectly normal. If, linguistically speaking, you are not at the 'joining in' stage, try to make yourself useful by quickly clearing any extraneous glasses and/or pouring more wine. Then sit back, relax and enjoy the show.

Unusual Tastes

Get used to eating things you don't normally eat. One of the best parts of travel is tasting strange delicacies you've never tried before. If you're a picky eater, vegetarian or vegan, don't look. If, however, you're the adventurous type, it'd be a crime not to sample some of the following culinary delights:

Lapin - Rabbit

Les viande de chaval - Horsemeat

Des béatilles - Organ meats

Steak Tartare - Finely chopped raw beef

Les pied de couchon - Pig's feet

Crette de coq - Rooster's combs

Le boudin - Blood sausage/pudding

Le sang - Blood

Le gésier - Gizzards

Cuisses de grenouilles - Frogs' legs (my father-in law remembers fishing the little critters straight from the river when he was a boy and selling any surplus at local restaurants).

Escargot - Garden snails

Le rognon - Kidneys

La langue - Tongue

Canard - Duck (cooked and packed in its own fat)

Des algues - Seaweed

Foie Gras - Specifically fattened goose or duck liver

Anguilee - Eel

La Cervelle - Brains

Des abats - Giblets

Oursins - Sea urchins - during the season just before December, the creatures are caught straight from the Sea, opened up with a pair of scissors (kind of looks like a decapitation ceremony without there being a head) and eaten raw, right there on the beach/rocks with fresh bread, butter and loads of dry white wine to wash them down.

Having said that, I admit I'm predominantly vegetarian, but do, on occasion succumb. For fully-fledged vegetarians who may be reconsidering their visa applications at this point, don't fret. There *is* hope and we'll get to that a little later.

The French Diet

There are practically millions of books, articles and other information available on this topic. People seem endlessly fascinated as to why French women don't get fat even though they eat bread, cheese and drink wine. And rightly so. Not only are they not fat, they are, generally speaking super svelte no matter what their physical age. Grrrr.

Statistically speaking, only 11 percent of the French population are obese compared to 30 percent of Americans and one in two Australians. But how is it possible that with all that fatty cheese being consumed (an estimated 40 pounds of cheese each year per person!) there's so little heart disease?

A paradox it seems? Perhaps. Though, I suspect the explanation may just be in the red wine, which among other 'national slimming secrets' reduces the risk of heart disease. As for their other dietary 'secrets' -straightforward common sense is what it's all about. Let's take a peep:

- The French practice portion control (think quality not quantity).
- They drink water instead of juice and sugary sodas (flushes toxins, keeps you hydrated and looking young).
- They walk everywhere (leave the car at home and walk, climb stairs, cycle).
- They cook their meals from scratch (no takeaway dinners with nasty chemical additives and mystery sauces gulped down in front of the TV).
- They eat a variety of foods and incorporate all food groups to keep things interesting, choosing high quality, seasonal and fresh produce instead of processed junk.
- They snack on fruit and yoghurt instead of candy bars.
- Not being a nation that believes in deprivation, they do eat desert, but the portions are small, not 'super-sized'.

Gourmet School Lunches

The food culture doesn't stop when it comes to the 'little' French people. Schools in France make sure to include balanced meals at lunchtime while at the same time introducing the kids to French cuisine. Hence, a 3-course meal for a 3 year old in France is nothing out of the ordinary.

Regardless of the fact that France is also infiltrated by fast food giants and obesity is slowly on the rise, the national food culture is instilled in them at a very young age. It seems from the moment they 'pop' out into the world, French children instinctively know that eating is a pleasure and that mealtimes are not only for ingesting food but also for sharing time and conversation.

One can expect to pay around €4 for a kid's school lunch in Paris and around €2 per plate in regional areas. That's around the same price as a burger and fries but the comparison stops there. For starters, all the produce is locally grown, everything is made by hand.

A sample school menu (which changes on a daily basis) can look something like this:

Entrée: Salade de tomate mozzarella

Main course: Poulet Basquaise avec Riz

Dessert: Crème caramel

Not too shabby, huh?

> "Tell me what you eat, and I will tell you what you are."
> Jean Anthelme Brillat-Savarin

Getting served in a café or restaurant (don't make me laugh!)

Sitting in my favorite café in Marseille around a year ago, I noticed a German couple at the table next to mine waiting patiently for the waiter to come by. As is usual practice around here, they where ignored for around 20 minutes. The waiter did pass by, several times in fact, but still managed to ignore them.

Even though they looked as though they had the patience of Saints, I did notice some subtle head shaking action and whispers under their breath. Eventually they'd had enough, got up, (while continually shaking their heads) and left.

I was tempted to stop them and tell them the following:

Wait ! That's just how it is around these parts. Don't take it personally. Sit, wait, and chill back. Eventually you *will* be served.

But I didn't.

At the time I felt as though they needed to find out for themselves. To serve their time like the rest of us (kind of nasty of me I know). But here's the thing. I know exactly why tourists get upset over this. For one, the service is nothing like it is back home. For another, I think there's a bit of a 'victim' mentality at play here. People take it personally because they are here to spend their hard earned dollars and nobody cares. This is partly true and partly false.

It's false because; believe me, the French get bad service too. And it's true because France is the world's most visited country. Therefore, they don't *need* to care. They know that the tourists will keep on coming back.

Fabrice tells me that this 'consider yourself lucky if you're served' phenomenon is known as *jmenfoutisme* (I don't care-ism). See what I have to put up with? How does one live, much less survive with a jemenfoutiste?

Bottom line; don't expect the same service you get back home because that's never going to happen. Call it rude, call it whatever you like, but the fact is, in France, the customer is not always right.

Point in case: An ordinary chore such as standing in line at the post office can be fraught with a bunch of fear on the customers' part. Like fear in terms of whether or not one will be able to gauge the current mood of the public servant. And one never can tell if the seemingly simple act of buying a postage stamp will be accompanied by a multitude of 'impossibilities'.

Like what?

Oh, I don't know. Perhaps they've stopped making stamps that day; perhaps the guy that delivers the stamps is on strike. Perhaps they're sitting in the backroom in a box and haven't been unpacked. Perhaps the public servant is due for his or her cigarette-break any second and can't be bothered with your 'unreasonable' request.

An ordinary appeal can turn into a major headache if you're not prepared to make like the French, shrug it off and put it down to the luck of the draw/customer/day. If you think I'm joking, just you wait, Henry Higgins, just you wait.

Remember these words as you wait in line. As you observe someone who happened to be standing behind you for an hour push in front (common practice) and consequently get served before you do. Don't even bother trying to bring up the injustice with the person behind the counter. It is, after all not his or her problem. You, however, are now faced with 2 choices: either put up a fight or get over it.

TIP: I asked Fabrice if he knew of any special 'insider' tricks to get better service in cafés, etc. At first he gave me the French shrug and shook his head (as if I was asking something otherworldly), then suddenly out of the blue he said…

"*Bah oui*…there is one thing you can do. Try to speak French. That may help a little."

Yeah right. Whether or not it helps, who knows, but at least you'll be able to understand what the waiter is hissing at you (through thin and bitter lips) under his breath.

Tips when out in a restaurant

- Close your menu when you're ready to order (or else the waiter doesn't care/come)
- Put together your knife and fork when you're done (consequences as above)
- Ask for the bill when you want to go (or else you'll be sitting there all bloody day or night).
- When ordering in a restaurant it's perfectly fine to ask for tap water, which is safe to drink. (Being too embarrassed won't do your wallet any favors).
- Ice cubes in rosé are the norm, a Marseille tradition in fact, due to the warmer climate.
- Ordering a carafe of wine in a restaurant is cheaper and still a very drinkable thing to do. (Ask for a quarter, half or large 'pichet').

Terribly Useful Vocabulary

I'm hungry: *jai faim*

I'm thirsty: *jai soif*

I would like some wine: *Je voudrais du vin*

Enjoy your meal: *Bon appétit*

Asking for the bill: *l'addition sil vous plais*

Surviving France as a Vegetarian

If you don't eat meat or any other animal products you definitely need a sense of humor because the French are a little behind in these matters. What's more, they just don't 'get it'. Be prepared to feel like an alien whenever you ask for a vegetarian option. Don't even try to explain why you are a vegetarian to begin with. Best to say it's a 'lifestyle choice' and leave it at that. That way you won't offend the meat eaters, provoke war or worse - perplexed blank stares into the distance.

Each time you're served a meal that contains only 'a little bit of meat' that's when you'll need to grab that previously mentioned sense of humor. Same with seafood, which they naturally think all vegetarians, eat.

Even when you give the waiter the third degree about the dish, and he or she insists it is 'meat free', you may still find suspicious looking animal products floating in the sauce. Often it's best to call the restaurant beforehand, explain you don't eat anything with a face. Ask for *'pas de viande, pas de poisson'* and hope for the best.

And even then, if you are **guaranteed** some vegetarian options, no doubt, you will still need to keep that humor.

Best option: Salad.

Second best: If you don't want to starve to death or die of boredom, it's probably best to cook and eat at home.

A guide to vegetarian/organic restaurants throughout France can be found at:

Laplage

http://www.laplage.fr/Accueil/

Despite the fact that France is not the most forward veggie-friendly country in the world, things are slowly getting better by the day. Luckily there's an abundance of fresh seasonal produce to choose from. Together with a little insight and planning, I promise, you will survive.

Here's a link to some Vegetarian French Recipes:

http://www.theveggietable.com/recipes/frenchrecipes.html

That way if you invite your new French neighbors for apero or dinner you'll be able to feed them something that won't totally alienate them.

Here's another:

http://www.food.com/recipes/french-vegetarian

More veggie-friendly/vegan links:

L'Association Végétarienne de France

http://www.vegetarisme.fr/

Mangez Vegetarien

http://www.mangez-vegetarien.com/

Véganisme

http://www.vegan.fr/

VegMag

http://www.vegmag.fr/

Veggie Cheese

Cheese lovers rejoice! It is possible to find vegetarian cheeses that use synthetic rennet instead of animal rennet (derived from stomachs of slaughtered animals). Possible, but not easy due to hit and miss labeling. It's not always clear as to whether or not they contain rennet. Therefore, better to discount the following labels, which are definitely known to contain animal rennet :

- Label Rouge
- Appellation d'Origine Controlée (AOC)
- Indication Géographique Protegée (IGP)

The following vegetarian manufacturer websites are said to contain detailed ingredients listings of their products and much more:

Paysange

http://www.paysange.com/

CuisineVegetarienne

http://www.cuisinevegetarienne.com/index.php?do_id=12

Aside from the above, look out for the following vegetarian-friendly indicators on labels.

- présure
- 100 percent vegetal
- Convennient aux végétariens

Alternately, order some of your favorite products online if they deliver in France. Or shop from English speaking / British shops which are gaining more and more popularity due to their stricter labeling requirements.

Vegetarian Dogs and Cats

Information on veggie food for dogs and cats is available at Zooplus http://www.zooplus.fr/

and Alternature http://www.alternature.com/

Organic Food Stores

Luckily these are on the increase. For your basic vegetarian and/or organic products track down the nearest health store (magasin BIO) in your area. Some popular organic food store chains are:

La Vie Claire

http://www.lavieclaire.com/

Bio-coop

http://www.biocoop.fr/

Bio-monde

http://www.biomonde.fr/

Naturalia

http://www.naturalia.fr/

If there's nothing in your area, most supermarkets have a small BIO (organic food) section where you'll find tofu, organic grains, soy products and other basic essentials.

True, the French are a little slow on the uptake with all things veggie/organic, but in the last few years I have seen big changes in an effort to rectify this. There's a huge increase in interest in relation to anything BIO and you can see it everywhere. From cafés, restaurants, shops, and TV programs. I suppose in the end, if the demand is there, people will have to listen.

Pass The Real Fromage!

"A country producing almost 360 different types of cheese cannot die."

(Winston Churchill)

Like mold on Roquefort, the cheese obsession definitely grows on you. French cheese is impressive and addictive. And for the French, their 400 different sorts of cheese are as essential, as drawing breath.

Supermarkets and market stalls displaying giant cheese counters are a sight to behold. You'll be overwhelmed by choice, which for the uninitiated can feel like a dairy deluge. In an effort to choose the 'right' cheese, I used to stand in the cold section (of the supermarket) and stare fixedly until my eyes glazed over. Luckily I don't do that anymore because I now have my anti-frostbite, steady staples. What are they? Glad you asked!

If you stock up on the following:

- Fourme d'ambert
- Roquefort
- Rustique
- Le Comté
- St Marcellin (goat's cheese)
- Cantal

…you really can't go wrong. And yes, you'll need a variety on hand to assure the cheese tray is constantly stocked for possible drop-in guests.

French Cheeses 101

Though there are hundreds of varietal cheeses, they can be classified into seven basic categories.

1. White mould cheeses (Camembert, Brie)
2. Blue cheeses (Roquefort, Fourme d'ambert)
3. Hard cheeses (Compté, Beaufort)
4. Uncooked semi-hard cheeses (Raclette, Tomme, Morbier)
5. Washed rind cheeses (the heavinly stinky Munster, Livarot, Epoisses, Pont-l'Eveque)
6. Goat milk cheeses (Fleur du Maquis, Rocamadour, Soignon)
7. Sheep milk cheeses (Ossau-Iraty)

Cheese serving tips:

- Taste depends mainly on seasons.
- Don't remove rinds before serving because it could offend the cheese connoisseurs.
- Cheeseboard variety is essential for pleasing everybody.
- Always serve with a variety of flavored breads and butter.
- There are different ways, and methodologies when it comes to cutting up the cheeses. For example round, soft cheeses are always cut up like cakes (When in doubt serve whole and let the experts lead the way).
- Try and partner the cheese with wine from the same region of origin.
- For example, blue cheese fares well with a light red like Morgon. Soft cheese with Médoc, Pomerol, Chinon.
- You get the point I'm sure, and there's no need to take any of this too seriously. What's more, by the time the cheese is served most people are more than likely too pickled to care.
- Always trust your cheese vendor's advice because *bien sure*, it will be spot on. He/she wants you to come back after all.

"A dinner which ends without cheese is like a beautiful woman with only one eye."

(Jean Anthelme Brillat-Savarin)

Wine

Some time ago, I watched a classic old French movie set in central France. The story revolved around two old peasant farmers and their simple daily lives. In one of the scenes, they ate the previous day's bone-dry bread and washed it down with some rough red wine. For breakfast! Nothing unusual I'm told. A 'heart starter', before the day's work.

In France, wine is considered a health beverage and generally drunk every day, which is probably why they produce 8 billion bottles per year. Whether you're a wine drinker or not, it's pretty hard to ignore this phenomenon when statistically speaking, women in France are expected to live at least 84 years - the longest life expectancy alongside their Japanese sisters. The men, on average, live 7 years less. Not a bad run, wouldn't you agree?

The antioxidant compound in grape skins (resveratrol) is said to be responsible. (Not that the French will stop themselves long enough to ask the why's and how's, preferring to leave that up to us – the baffled onlookers).

But where does one draw the line? Wine with lunch, during l'heure d'apéro and dinner is a given. Even at Marseille's IKEA, the Swedish furniture giant's restaurant, I watched in awe as people grabbed a glass or small carafe of wine as an accompaniment to their braised octopus. Wine, instead of water. Given these lifestyle circumstances it's easy to see how one could turn into a lush.

Think about it: If the western standard of no more than 2 glasses of wine per day stands fast then we're in fact dealing with a nation of functioning alcoholics. Needless to say, after 2 years of living here, I went on a 5-month liver cleanse/detox just to prove to myself that I wasn't one of them. It worked. For a while.

Apéro time, an unavoidable national institution will eventually track you down. The irresistible hour or two of guzzling alcohol and eating snacks before the actual meal starts at 6pm sharp. Even though I don't wear a watch, I know this because it's the only time of day anybody looks at his or hers in France. What can I say? The statistics speak for themselves.

French Wine 101

Traditionally French wine is blended from various grape varieties that are associated with specific regions such as Cabernet Sauvignon from Bordeaux, Syrah from Rhone etc.

Wine Regions

Loire – white wine region that covers a great distance along the Loire River through central and western France. Varieties and styles vary.

Champagne – eastern France near Belgium and Luxembourg is the coldest wine region and therefore perfect for the bubbly (white and rosé). The French are pretty possessive about their sparkly and will not allow anybody else around the world to call their (international) sparkling wine 'Champagne'. To be blessed with this honorable title, the grapes must be grown in the Champagne region. And the wine must be produced in line with the traditional method known as Methode Champenoise.

Bordeaux - along the Atlantic coast produces red wine blends from Merlot, Cabernet Sauvignon and Cabernet Franc. Also some dry and sweet wines such as Chateau d'Yquem.

Alsace – in eastern France borders with Germany. Known as a white-wine region, it produces dry, fresh and fruity wines. Also some red, rosé, sparkling and sweet wines.

Burgundy or Bourgogne - in eastern France produces red wine made from Pinot Noir, and white from Chardonnay.

Rhone – a red wine region in southeastern France. Varietals differ depending on the region of the Rhone River, as in the southern or northern part.

Provence – southeast region next to the Mediterranean is the warmest wine region, well known for producing excellent rosé and red wine.

Languedoc-Roussillon – large wine area known for producing cheap, bulk wines. Most of the area's wine is sold as *Vin de Pays d'Oc*.

Jura – small mountainous wine region near Switzerland. Also known for its Burgundy, Chardonnay and Pinot Noir varieties and unique wine styles Vin de Paille and Vin Jaune.

Savoy – white wine region in the Alps near Switzerland produces grapes unique to this region.

South West France – known for a diverse mix of grapes/areas. The red wine is similar to the Bordeaux. Some areas also produce dry reds as well as sweet white wines.

Corsica – known for strong wines. The island is however still developing their production methods and different varietal styles. Three leading grape varieties are Sciacarello, Vermentino and Nielluccio (also known as the spice wine of France).

> "Burgundy makes you think off silly things, Bordeaux makes you talk of them and Champagne makes you do them".
>
> (Anthelme Brillat-Savarin)

Reading French wine labels

The *'Appelation'* is the name for the growing area where the wine comes from, followed by a single vineyard designation.

The *'Négociant'* is the name of the wine maker (a single wine maker or a company).

The *'Varietal'* is the 'type' of grape

The *'Vintage'* is the year of production

Pairing French wine with food

The archaic rule is red wine goes with red meat and white wine with seafood and poultry. However these days that's irrelevant. The emphasis is on pleasure and enjoyment of the wine and I think it's fair to say the French aren't big on rules anyway so you can drink whatever you like.

If, however, you prefer some sort of guideline, it's actually not too complicated. First you'll need to determine whether or not the wine is light, rich, sweet or spicy so you can pair the wine with food that equals its intensity. In other words, try to match the weight of the wine with the weight of the food.

Hints:

Red Bordeaux with lamb

Beaujolais with pork

Pinot Noir with duck, salmon

Cabernet Sauvignon with grilled meat, beef, venison

Burgundy with game, braised meat

Zinfandel with turkey, pheasant and/or quail

Sauvignon Blanc with oysters, shrimps

Chardonnay with chicken, lobster, scallops

Sauternes with blue cheese

Champagne with appetizers, deserts or cheese (anytime's a good time for the Bubbly)

"A meal without wine is like a day without sunshine"
Anthelme Brillat-Savarin

Food and Politics

(a perfect mélange)

Fabrice tells me the French talk about food because, really, nothing else is as important. And they talk about politics when nothing is on their plate. Evidently, the politicians in France understand that if people have nothing on their plates, heads will once again be chopped!

Good point, but bear in mind the above applies not only to a lack of food but also the quality and nutritional value of the food.

Unlike the US and Australia for example, France does not support Genetically Modified food (labeled as GM or GMO overseas and OGM here). Strict regulations apply. For example, if any shelved products in France contain GM food this must be clearly labeled on the packaging. Even so, you will be hard-pressed to find any GM food at all.

It's the same story with fluoridated tap water. Here, it simply doesn't exist. Why? It's against government policy because it's toxic. That being so, one can't help but wonder why other countries allow it?

Please, don't take my word for it. If you're interested in learning more about health in general and/or what's in your food/water/medication check out http://www.mercola.com, which is (apparently) the world's number 1 health website.

Information on GMO foods:

http://gmo.mercola.com/

Information on fluoridated tap water:

http://fluoride.mercola.com/

It's no secret we no longer know what we are eating. Sadly, most of us are unaware that we're systematically poisoned on a daily basis. Frankly speaking, if our health alone is not enough incentive to move countries, I don't know what is.

Ever heard of José Bové? He's a national hero in France and no, he's not a sports star. Bové, a farmer, is an anti GMO activist who at one time was actually sent to jail because he cut down a field of genetically modified corn.

A radical, who doesn't 'wait for permission', he created a movement called la Confédération Paysanne, which is essentially a French farmers' union campaigning for peasant family farming, environmentally friendly agricultural methods and quality produce.

In fact, in 2007 Bové was a candidate for the presidency but with only 1.32 percent of voters in his pocket, clearly it wasn't enough to enter the game. Not big enough to become the new President perhaps, but it didn't stop him fighting GM giants like Monsanto and the like.

https://en.wikipedia.org/wiki/Monsanto

And that, my friends, is French mentality in a nutshell. They don't take lightly to being treated like sheep, being told what to do and last but never least, being told what to eat.

"Everything ends this way in France - everything. Weddings, christenings, duels, burials, swindlings, diplomatic affairs -everything is a pretext for a good dinner."

(Jean Anouilh)

Favorite Food Blogs:

Barbara Austin - "Eating, drinking and writing in Paris"

http://www.barbraaustin.com/

http://www.barbraaustin.com/category/paris-addresses/

Cannelle Vanille – "Food, Life and Photography" http://www.cannellevanille.com/

Chocolate & Zucchini – A food blog by a Parisian woman living in Montmartre

http://www.chocolateandzucchini.com/

David Lebovitz – A Californian chef "Living the sweet life in Paris" http://www.davidlebovitz.com/

Lucy's Kitchen Notebook – An author, photographer and foodie living in Lyon

http://www.kitchen-notebook.blogspot.com/

Lunch in the Loft – An artist-cook who gives cooking lessons from home

http://www.lunchintheloft.com/Lunch_in_the_Loft.html

http://www.frenchgirlcuisine.com/

Expat Isolation

"There are only two tragedies in life: One is not getting what one wants,

and the other is getting it".

(Oscar Wilde)

If you're going to be an expat or travel for an extended period of time you will experience periods of loneliness, isolation and culture shock. It's an aspect of long-term travel and/or relocation that helps build character. An unwelcome penalty that doesn't discriminate and can strike anybody at anytime.

Signs Of Culture Shock and/or Isolation

- Marital Stress
- Family conflict and/or tension
- Withdrawal from contact with locals (guilty)
- Homesickness
- Constant weeping (often unexplainable, and yes, guilty)
- Lack of motivation (yep)
- Psychosomatic illness (guilty)
- Obsessive-compulsive habits magnified (like constant cleaning, hand washing etc)
- Unable to work and/or concentrate
- Compulsive eating (tick)
- Weight gain (tick)
- Excessive drinking (tick)
- Spending excessive amounts of time reading and or surfing the Internet (guilty as charged)
- Excessive amounts of sleep

Not speaking the local lingo well or perhaps, like me, not at all in the beginning doesn't help. Apart from the language barrier per se, there are other, more subtle forms of communication (like being able to 'adequately' express one's feelings), which no longer apply once you move to the other side of the world.

For example when we speak to a friend, there are usually several layers within what's being said. There's the text, as in what is actually vocalized and then there's the subtext (or what is implied beneath the words). The lack of being able to communicate in a manner or language one is used to is frustrating to say the least. Like not being able to discuss in detail one's topic of expertise for instance. For me, that would be a piece of theater or film for example, (a specific language within a language).

Another thing that doesn't help is not knowing anybody aside from one's partner's immediate family and friends, which can make one feel like the stereotypical 'trailing spouse'.

Aside from the above, in many cases it's easy to get stuck in patterns of behavior, which unwillingly keep you from becoming a part of your new environment. Working via the Internet is one example.

An excerpt from one of my blog entries…

"Living on the other side of the world, away from family and friends can feel isolating at times. Especially at first, when you don't speak a word of the language - when occasionally you need to reach out to someone and there's nobody around. Your friends back home are wondering what the hell you're complaining about. Your husband's away on a long business trip and your highlight of the day is buying some tomatoes at the market for a bit of human contact via the person at the cash register…"

Admittedly, the above is written from the perspective of a 40-something introvert who is not a group person or a 'joiner' - or particularly social for that matter. From time to time (albeit short periods of time), I actually do crave people but generally speaking, unless I'm forced into some kind of situation that requires participation, I don't do it.

During my first year or so in France an invitation to a casual BBQ on a Sunday afternoon seemed like a logistic nightmare. I'd break out in a sweat at the mere thought of being surrounded by a bunch of French people - convinced they would find my lack of linguistic skill far from palatable.

Plus I started to resent having to depend on Fabrice for everything. Constantly translating. Interpreting. I have to say he always did his best to translate my un-translatable, trashy one-liners; still, nobody laughed. How does one cope in these situations? One way is to embrace the circumstances at hand. Another is to retreat and look around for a cracking good bottle of Rosé. I opt for the second choice.

Whatever, that's the way I'm wired. Maybe you are too, but even so; don't do what I did and hide for the first year. Try and make an effort to get out of the house. Talk to people, go for long walks, take photos, sit in a café and write letters, go to a movie, an art gallery, a bar, stroll the markets. Even tiny bits of daily communication help to gain confidence.

By the same token, whether or not you are a solitary creature by choice is irrelevant. There will be times when you're faced with an illness or a crisis, which is when the isolation hits you the most. When you need help and you're suddenly alone with no family or friends to turn to. Don't forget, being an expat is a full time job. You get to live it all day and every day, and I'm afraid it doesn't get more personal than that.

(More) Integration Tips From The Introvert

Learn the language: As previously mentioned, this one's really the most important point. Do yourself a huge favor and make this your priority. Being extremely slow on the uptake, I know what I speak of. My husband is French but he speaks English, which is generally what we speak when we're together. What this meant was that I had no immediate need to learn French, so I didn't. Now, 3 years later, I'm able to 'get by', but what's taken me 3 years to learn (via osmosis most likely), I could have learned in 1 year or less.

Unless you speak the language everything can take on the tone of 'too hard'. For example, something that would normally be a 2-minute job in your native country takes an eternity in France. It's exhausting; even if you're husband or wife is French it doesn't make all that much difference. Most certainly, you'll be relying on them to do stuff for you at the beginning, but you will eventually want to stop doing that. Why? Not only is it a burden on your spouse (though they most likely won't admit it), it's never good to feel as though you've lost your independence. Right?

Get out of the house: If you happen to be a writer or work online in another medium, schedule a day when you go to a café and work where people are. Some places offer wireless like Starbucks, Virgin Bookstore and McDonalds, all alive, well, and thriving in France. So are plenty of other, more interesting options.

Hang out with your kids: If you have children you're in luck because it forces you to automatically be more entwined with whatever activities, be it school or extracurricular, they happen to be involved in (whether they like it or not).

Joining clubs and expat associations: In a way it's probably not ideal to cling to your own kind in an effort to integrate. On the other hand it can be comforting. Especially when it's people who understand what you're going through and are more likely to help you when you really need help.

Make an extra effort to **stay in touch with friends and family.** If you're not computer savvy, you need to get with the times and make friends with gadgets. I'm far from being a computer whiz but I have to admit that making friends with modern technology was a good personal investment. Today, I can't imagine life without the Internet, and/or skype. Apart from making it easy to stay in touch with loved ones, my laptop has given me an opportunity to earn a living whilst indulging my travel habits. Theoretically, it means I can be and live location independent and that my friends, spells freedom with a capital 'F'. Priceless.

Get a hobby: As soon as possible, try to get back into doing whatever you were doing at home, sports, yoga, martial arts, whatever it was; If you didn't have any hobbies or special interests then it's never too late to learn a new skill; cook, paint, make ceramics, take up Argentinean tango, join a walking group. There are no limits when you're in the midst of building a new life.

Going home from time to time is a good way of reaffirming why you left in the first place. It'll quickly put things into perspective and (most likely) make you realize that things in your newly adopted home aren't so bad after all. Be prepared for a lack of sympathy. When you chat with your family and friends and tell them that it's actually trying from time to time, they probably won't believe you. Why should they? After all, you are 'living the dream'. And more often than not, you're also living 'their dream'.

I don't want to disguise the facts. The early adjustment period of being in a new place is difficult. Unfortunately it's not all about sipping coffees on sidewalk terraces all day long. The effort it takes to settle in a new place will reap rewards in the end. But you'll need determination, a lot of guts and some time. Would I do it all over again? In a heartbeat.

"If the world turns its back on you, pinch it in the @ss"

(web wisdom)

Dating In France

(A tale of everyday seduction)

"Quit your job .

Buy a ticket.

Get a tan.

Fall in love.

Never return"

(Spencer Antle)

Ahhh! The seduction practices à la Française. Why are we so intrigued? We're constantly told the French are romantic, complex but charming, passionate, elegant, volatile, playful, cheeky, sometimes maddening but always fascinating. The French have a big reputation to uphold, that's for sure. And if you've read this far then I suppose you'd like to know if it's all true.

Very well then…

Truth be told, albeit fascinating, it's not always easy being married to a person from a different heritage. There are challenges, communication issues and cultural differences to overcome. Having said that, I wholeheartedly feel the positives of a cross-cultural relationship far outweigh any seeming negatives. It's exciting, keeps one on one's tippy toes and it sure as hell beats monotony.

I met Fabrice a few years ago at a seedy bar in Sydney, Australia. After our initial meeting I ran away. Twice, in fact. Why? Well apart from being self-conscious and not wanting him to see my strange looking feet, I was intimidated. He had the kind of confidence I admired and simultaneously feared. He was self-assured, direct, charming and charismatic and apart from being French, he was unlike any other person I'd ever met.

His lifestyle, beliefs, philosophy and overall 'lightness of being' continuously sweet-talking me to surrender to the moment, the 'now', until six months or so later, he literally seduced me out of my shell and lured me to France.

Needless to say, meeting Fabrice proved to be a major turning point in my life.

- Just because you don't 'think' you've fallen head over heals for someone from the start doesn't mean you haven't.
- Just because you're confused, unsure of yourself or the other person, doesn't mean they're not right for you.

Too many of us are looking for some sort of 'type'. And if we don't happen to find that narrow standard 'type' of person, we're not interested - thereby unknowingly short-circuiting possible new experiences, life paths, chapters and/or the chance of falling in love.

Most of my single 40-something girlfriends in Australia can't seem to meet a decent man. I'm not exactly sure why, but I do have some idea. Generally speaking, the Australian male is obsessed by young women. Apart from that, he is somewhat self-conscious, timid and emotionally repressed when it comes to dealing with the opposite sex (obviously not the case in France).

To clarify, I'm not here to psychoanalyze or denigrate Australian men, nor do I mean any disrespect. I'm speaking from a general point of view (as well as personal experience). Ultimately, comparing the Australian male to the French male is futile because you're essentially dealing with a completely different species. Chalk and cheese.

I'm simply attempting to demonstrate that there is hope. That it's possible to find true love - even if you're an oddball introvert on the far side of 40. And above all else, what I'm saying here is this: If you can't find love in your own backyard, you need to look over the fence. Sometimes way beyond!

That's right. One cannot subsist on meat-pies alone my friends. If you can't meet Mr Right at home, go to France (or Italy for that matter); sit at a café by yourself – guaranteed, five minutes later you won't be by yourself anymore. Be on guard, be assertive but at the same time try and keep an open frame of mind.

Flirting - the national pastime

Everybody flirts. It's part of the entertainment in France. An ordinary trip to the supermarket can be a sensual experience. People look at one another. Men check out women. Women check out men. It is not offensive to look. It's almost expected. If the attention is unwanted it is simply ignored. No drama.

French women in particular have a leeway on flirting. However, generally speaking they don't make eye contact unless they're interested and want to initiate contact. If a French woman is not interested she won't bother being 'nice' about it. She simply cuts you off. This is why foreign women usually get hassled, because they don't know the rules of the game.

What's more, the French don't have the need to 'define the relationship' after a few dates. In France ambiguity is just fine. No need for clarification. It is as it is. Don't get too heavy or too serious. Keep it light. Enjoy the food, the wine and the conversation. Retain a little mystery, flirt and soak up the ambience. If you keep it simple there's really no need to have 'the talk', wanting to know whether or not you're on the same page. Who cares!

In France, you'll know things are getting *sérieux* if your French darling takes you home to meet *les parents*. That's usually a pretty good indicator. As a rule, tying the knot is not at the forefront of the French mind. Around 48 percent of French men and women live together and have children sans the stress about making things 'official'. Often, if and when they finally do get married it's for mutually beneficial tax reasons. And I know what you're thinking. Where's the romance in that? I agree.

But sometimes I have to wonder if it's not more romantic <u>not</u> to get married. At least you know the person genuinely wants to be with you instead of being forced to hang around.

But I digress. As one would expect, changing countries and starting a new life is an exciting experience, but it can also feel lonely. We've already established it's not easy starting over in a new place, with friends and family and everything familiar on the other side of the world. I imagine, it would be all the more challenging as a single person.

The Old-Fashioned Way

Being an old-fashioned girl at heart, I still believe in meeting people by chance, though I suppose these days, those types of encounters are somewhat antiquated. I also believe in the art of archaic introductions via friends, which is ironically how it works in France a lot of the time, so be sure to always take up those dinner invitations, aperitifs, BBQ's, parties etc.

Expat Clubs and Associations

Another way to meet people (who lead to other people) is to get involved in some of the expat clubs/groups and different associations.

http://www.americancommunityinfrance.com/american-clubs-and-organizations-for-expatriates-in-france/

You will find similar lists of expat groups on British, Australian, and Canadian consulate websites. Alternatively, check with your local mairie (town hall) for information on various French newcomers' associations. That way, even if you don't speak a word of French you'll at least be mingling.

Tip from Fabrice: If you want to meet someone decent, go out during the week not on the weekend. Why? He says the weekends are for the masses and that's when all the French losers head out.

I'm probably stating the obvious here, but don't be too blatant if you're looking to 'hook up' or get married. It's not a good look in any country or situation and people can smell desperation a mile off. Especially here. It's no secret people want a European passport. At any cost it seems.

Not too long ago, I received an email asking if I knew of someone who is willing to get married for a bit of extra cash. Goes without saying that I don't and even if I did I wouldn't say so. Still, it's a sign of the times we live in. Each to their own and all of that but I honestly think this kind of approach is unnecessary and probably won't serve you in the long run. So if you want my advice, keep it simple, keep it pure.

Start by socializing and staying open and friendly with the aim of 'getting to know people'. If you approach the whole thing without 'agenda' you never know what's around the corner. Think, "If it's meant to be…", a pretty good philosophy to adopt around these parts - and one the French themselves probably invented.

Another good approach is to take a class or course in something that interests you. Learning French or participating in a language exchange group is probably a good place to start, or else volunteer.

Online Dating

France may be the country of dreams and romance. Paris may well be the city of love. But if she's not delivering the results you'd hoped for, you may want to get with the contemporary beat and check out some French dating sites. Who knows? Chances are you could find your soul mate before you even leave your country of residence.

Admittedly, I've never used any of these sites; hence I am not an authority on them or on the topic of online dating. That being so, just in case any of these are not what they say they are, don't shoot the messenger. It goes without saying that millions of less desirable characters frequent the Internet, so please be sure to properly check out any future prospects before you arrange an actual date.

A while ago I received another email from an American woman who'd met a French man online. Even though they'd never met in real life, she said he'd professed his undying love and wanted to marry her just as soon as she stepped off the plane in France. Meanwhile she asked him for his phone number and he kept avoiding the topic. In over 6 months of online dating, she never got his number or his actual address.

Basically she wrote to ask if this was normal behavior in French culture. I wrote back and told her to be careful. This was obviously not 'normal' coming from a Frenchman (or anyone else for that matter). Usually they whip out their number before you've even said hello – regardless of whether or not you want it.

Nevertheless, online dating is definitely gaining in popularity around these parts and with this, just as with anything else, the French are blasé and take things in their stride. Just the other day I talked to a young couple at a family BBQ. When I asked them how they met..."Internet", they said, without hesitation.

Only a few years ago, admitting one met via the Internet seemed a little out of the ordinary, artificial, somewhat desperate and perhaps not ideal. Today it is the norm. For sure, online dating does present some advantages. You get to check out someone's profile, basic likes, dislikes or 'psycho' tendencies right away without the 'surprise' package further down the track.

That being so, there's certainly no harm in looking…or perhaps even establishing a friendship with someone who may not quite fit your romantic ideal. Right? Just make sure to play it safe - it's no secret that some people on the Internet can only be characterized as "loons".

To give you a taste of what's out there in French cyberspace, I 'link'collected via the local TV, radio, Internet and magazines. I dare say if you do your own search you might even find better (albeit less popular) options. Most of the sites are in English, some only in French.

Popular Internet Dating Sites

eDarling

http://www.edarling.fr/

AttractiveWorld

http://www.attractiveworld.net/

Meeticaffinity

http://www.meeticaffinity.fr/

Meetic

http://www.meetic.fr/

France Dating (dating service for singles)

http://www.connectingsingles.com/free_dating_online/france_free_dating_online.htm

Metrodate

http://www.metrodate.com/france/

Loveawake

http://www.loveawake.com/free-online-dating/France-dating-service.html

Datememateme

http://www.datememateme.com/dating/france

Rencontre France

http://www.rencontre-france.eu/

Dome Recontre

http://www.domeconnection.com/en/france-serious-dating.html

Dating sites by regions:

Dating Service

http://www.dating-service.com/Sites/Regions/france/

Speed Dating

If you prefer to check out any future relationship prospects in the flesh, the concept of Speed and Turbo dating (Soiréés Speed Dating) hit France a number of years ago. To some, perhaps, the whole speed-dating thing can seem a little impersonal and fast food-ish, but if you're the kind of individual who doesn't like to waste precious time, they're probably a pretty good bet. Click below for more information:

http://www.turbo-dating.com/

Meeting like-minded people

If you're not necessarily looking for a partner, here's a great website for meeting people and expanding your circle of friends according to your interests. No need to go to the "movies, theater, hiking, Japanese restaurant" by yourself anymore. If you simply want to connect with like-minded individuals, here's a link :

http://www.onvasortir.com/

Notes on 'Dating'

The French generally don't 'date' as we understand the term 'dating' to mean. People tend to go out in groups and then kind of hook up with each other on a casual basis. Afterwards, if there's anything more to it (post hook up), chances are the hooker-uppers won't tell you they've hooked up or that they're an item, preferring to practice discretion and secrecy about these things.

So the concept of 'dating' is basically unheard of.

For example, French women are proud, confident and mysterious. They are not as open as American or Australian women, preferring to meet men at dinner parties within groups etc. If they do meet a guy for a drink, it is just that, not necessarily a date. If you ask them about dating, they actually don't 'get it' and find the whole idea tedious. Why? Because they don't need permission to have a drink with someone or to sleep with someone they like.

Basically, if the guy doesn't call, French women don't get upset or hung up on him for months or years. If he doesn't call he's simply not worth it and five minutes later he is forgotten. Instead of getting hung up, they trust their instincts and intuit what's going on. That being so, they don't need to read certain best selling self-help books (which shall remain nameless) to know whether or not someone is 'into them' or not.

> "French women have been made beautiful by the French people - they're very aware of their bodies, the way they move and speak, they're very confident of their sexuality. French society's made them like that."
>
> (Charlotte Rampling)

Sexually speaking, French women are just as aggressive as the men. Difference being, they're a lot subtler about these things. However, it is still generally the men who actively pursue. Good thing is, French men don't wait to call you and they don't play hard to get. They simply call. Isn't that lovely?

By the way, if you'd like to read more about French men and what makes them tick, I've got you covered in **'French Men on Love & Women',** available right here: https://www.amazon.com/dp/B01M184PUI

Speaking of which, here's another agreeable fact…

9 out of 10 French women are sexually active over the age of 50. Those statistics alone should be enough reason to pack your bags !!!

Undeniably, less hang ups, fewer inhibitions and sexual taboos often make for great dinner conversation - some things one hears or gets asked around the dinner table are so blatant; it's difficult (for the uninitiated) to know where to look or how to respond. But you'll soon get used to people going through your underwear drawer, even if you're not (yet) on a first name basis. And as far as your underwear is concerned, don't worry too much about folding your bits and pieces nice and neat; naturally, the French prefer things to be a little dishevelled.

Pleasure and Pain

The French take great pleasure in making us (mere mortals) squirm because, well, basically they think we're all too uptight. For example, for them, sex with 'friends' is a perfectly normal, natural and mutually beneficial, 'technical' arrangement. I suppose, these days most people and cultures around the world are aware of the term 'fuck-buddy'. Not groundbreaking news, right?

Even so, when faced with these types of ideas and organizations, it may take a little getting used to for the average (old-fashioned), non-French person. When, for instance, one meets one's partner's 'friends' in a social situation one can never be sure whether or not the line of friendship has been crossed - never mind with whom, when and how many times.

My advice? If you can't beat them, join them, or try not to think about it. I'm sorry my friends, but that's really the best I have. I'm afraid it's all part of the fun and games around these parts. And don't say I didn't warn you.

Last though by no means least I'd like to close this chapter with the following:

Infidelity and the French is a well-worn cliché, and even though infidelity exists (like anywhere else in the world), the myth of that being 'accepted' is only a myth. You may be happy to know, in reality; most French women (and men) generally won't tolerate any extramarital horizontal tango.

Tip: If you've never seen the film '2 days in Paris' (directed by, and starring Julie Delpy and Adam Goldberg), I recommend you do. Not only is it a great film, it's also funny and provides some brilliant insight into American/French cultural differences within the context of a mixed relationship.

Links for Paris lovers

52 Martinis – a guy on the hunt for the finest cocktails in Paris

http://www.52martinis.com/

Beth Arnold, "Letter from Paris" – an award-winning journalist living and writing in Paris

http://www.betharnold.com/

I prefer Paris – an ex New Yorker's inside guide to Paris

http://www.ipreferparis.typepad.com/

Girls Guide to Paris – the name says it all

http://www.girlsguidetoparis.com/

Hip Paris – an online hub for anything that's hot right now in the 'city of light' (food, fashion, architecture, culture, off the beaten path places, hip people, events)

http://www.hipparis.com/

Unlock Paris – Your insider guide to Paris

http://www.unlockparis.com/

La Mom Paris – "Tales of an American mom in Paris"

http://www.lamomparis.com/

Lost in Cheeseland – a blog about a girl from Philadelphia who fell in love with a French guy and moved to Paris

http://www.lostincheeseland.com/

One and Only Paris Photography – An American/French couple who are photographers in Paris http://www.oneandonlyparisphotography.com/

Paris by Appointments Only – "Your key to the city's hidden doors"

http://www.parisbao.com/

Paris Imperfect – a writer/dreamer who moved to France on a romantic whim. She blogs about the good and the bad

http://www.parisimperfect.wordpress.com/about/

Parisien Salon – a blog about the food, the scene, the style and fabulous finds in Paris

http://www.parisiensalon.com/

Prete Moi Paris – a blog about an American living in Paris

http://www.pretemoiparis.com/about/

Secrets of Paris – "Insider tips for living in Paris"

http://www.secretsofparis.com/

Chapter 4

Your Own Home In France

The best places to invest are not necessarily the best places to live. Vice versa. It all depends on what you're after. Clearly, you'll find the cheapest properties where there is the least demand, which is not always a reflection on the area itself. In some areas property is cheap simply because there is no work.

Good deals exist everywhere, so keep an open mind and be prepared to explore places other people might not even consider. For instance, some years back, one of Fabrice's friends bought an entire deserted village (in the Alps behind Nice) for under €35 000.

With France being highly diverse…rolling hills, flat lands, mountains, a fabulous coastline, the Atlantic and Mediterranean Seas, many rivers, ancient villages and cities of culture, the best place to live really depends on individual tastes. Plus there are many different regions, varying climates and variety in sizes of towns, villages and cities to consider.

One thing's for sure. With so many inexpensive properties available - from run down stone barns to medieval castles, village cottages and low maintenance beach apartments, somewhere in France, the ideal home is waiting for you.

Ideal for you might mean a stone cottage in rural apple blossom Normandy, a chalet in a forest, a rustic farmhouse on lush soil, a quaint village, a seaside villa in sunny Provence or an apartment of character in elegant Paris.

Before you plunge in, there are some points that need careful consideration. Living somewhere is an entirely different beast to spending a couple of months a year on vacation.

For starters, consider that France is divided into 26 regions (metropolitan France and Corsica) and 4 overseas territories (Réunion, Martinique, Guadeloupe, Guyana). The regions are subdivided into 100 départments (96 metropolitan and 4 overseas). That's a lot of choice.

Points to consider:

Where do you want to be? The sea, a tiny village, a city or a remote rural property far removed from the crowds? Do you want to be isolated or connected to a motorway, airport or harbor? Coast or inland? What about shops? Do you need them at walking or driving distance? Are you fussed about Internet access? Location? Perhaps you want to be near the border of Italy or Spain where you can pop over for some cheaper shopping.

What type of climate are you seeking? The Atlantic coast has a temperate climate with mild wet winters, cool summers and prevailing winds. The continental climate in the east means hot summers and cold winters, rain and snow in mountainous parts. Central France also experiences a continental climate while the Mediterranean coast enjoys hot dry summers, mild winters, (and rainfall over winter much like central France). Here's a link to the hours of sunshine per year for each region: http://www.the-france-page.com/france/annual-hours-of-sun.html

Do you want your property to be your new home, your second home during vacation, or year-round? Perhaps you are simply looking for an investment property as a steady stream of income? Maybe you're thinking of renting it to tourists or friends when you're not there, not using it?

Structurally speaking, are you happy to tackle some DIY restoration or would you prefer a place you can move into straight away?

Be prepared to do some legwork and make sure to **visit more that one region** to get an idea of diversity. Do the research. Each area of France is unique with it's own qualities and quirks, and as I said, prices in many regions are amazingly low. Before you set your heart on a particular region, try before you buy and rent (I'd say for a minimum of 3 to 6 months).

When you find a place, list the **positives and negatives.** What do you have to have? What's sort of important? What's not that important?

Ask questions about the area, the property, its history etc. A good property agent will be able to help.

Make sure you see the real thing - **never buy the property via the Internet.**

How will you **finance** your purchase? Need a mortgage? French mortgages have great rates, so make sure to shop around.

Think about your **currency exchange**. You can save money on your purchase (often thousands) if you secure your money at today's rate, protect yourself against unpredictable currency movements and purchase later with companies like SMART currency exchange. Here's more info: http://www.smartcurrencyexchange.com/

Don't rush into choosing the right place. Be objective and give yourself time before you make a final decision.

Remember at the moment **it's a buyers market,** putting you in a dominant position. Offering 10 to 15 percent below market price is perfectly acceptable. Renovations? Use it as a bargaining point.

When you find an agent, **be clear what you're looking for.** Give them a list of what you want. When you find a place, take 2-3 long visits to get a good feel for the place.

Always get independent advice.

Capital Gains Tax? If you're interested in learning about capital gains tax (laws fluctuate) here's a link:

https://www.french-property.com/guides/france/finance-taxation/taxation/capital-gains-tax/rate/

Your Real Estate Dream Come True

With the continuing decline of the euro and real estate prices, you couldn't pick a better time to arrive and thrive. As already mentioned in the cost of living chapter, with a bit of luck, your equity (the difference between what you owe the bank and your current property's value) could buy you a home in France.

In my case, the difference added up to $100 000 AUD (Australian dollars), which at the time worked out to be €60 000. Not a fortune by any means but more than enough to buy a piece of land with a small house in regional France, or a one-bedroom flat/studio in Marseille.

I've never understood why anybody would want to pay off a massive house for the rest of their days when they can own their own (albeit smaller) home right now - at a fraction of the price.

If you think you can't do small, think again…

I managed to adjust from a 200 m2 house in rural Australia with a quarter acre of land, to living in a 45m2 city apartment with balcony in France. In terms of 'size', I have never looked back (less maintenance, stress and worry = more freedom).

Freedom for less than €50 000

Here's what €50 000 (starting at €20 000) in the beautiful Languedoc-Roussillon region, (where the sun shines for more than 300 days per year) will buy you.

http://www.leboncoin.fr/ventes_immobilieres/offres/languedoc_roussillon?f=a&th=1&pe=2&ret=1&ret=2

Obviously these prices are for people who can look past the run down, shell and see the potential of a palace. And yes, the homes I speak of do require a bit of a face-lift, (some more than others), but who cares if you're surrounded by your own four walls. As long as the place is habitable, you can always renovate down the track.

Palace or shack, you've just bought your freedom, and that my friends, is irreplaceable.

On the opposite end of the spectrum, in Australia, the houses in suburbs keep getting bigger. Backyards keep getting smaller. In Victoria and New South Wales, the average house size is over 250m2. That's huge!

People are basically creating their entire world inside the safety of their walls, sacrificing precious outdoor space in order to extend living space. Becoming more insular by locking themselves inside, in the hope to escape what's going on outside. Needless to say if the houses are getting bigger, so are the mortgages and personal debt, which most people pay off for the rest of their lives.

Mortgage: In the word mortgage, the mort- is from the Latin word mori (via old French mort) for death and –gage is from the sense of that word meaning a pledge to forfeit something of value if a debt is not repaid. So mortgage is literally a death pledge.

Source : http://truedemocracyparty.net/2013/01/mortgage-death-pledge-latin-words-mort-gage-literally-translated-mort-means-death-gage-means-pledge/

Case in point : My mother lives in a 40m2 inner-city apartment in Melbourne. It is small, basic, and nothing extravagant but it's centrally located, which is reflected in its estimated value. If you want something bigger, and still semi-affordable (in Australia, it's difficult to find anything decent under half a million dollars) you need to move further out and live in an uninspiring, housing-estate-mortgage-factory.

I understand a lot of people actually like the suburbs because the uniform, square sameness of suburban Australia is non-threatening, which makes them feel secure (a false sense of safety driven by fear). Each to their own and all that, it's just sad that for some, it is all they've ever known and all they will ever know in their lifetime.

It doesn't have to be that way…

Friends back home are constantly amazed when I tell them how little it costs to buy a provincial house with land, or an apartment in a gorgeous part of France. The reason they can't believe it is because it sounds too good to be true. Simply put, home ownership has become unreachable in most parts of the world.

Need more inspiration?

Apartments under €50 000 (starting at 40m2) in the Midi-Pyrénéés. Here's what I found:

http://www.leboncoin.fr/ventes_immobilieres/offres/midi_pyrenees/?f=a&th=1&pe=2&sqs=5&ret=2

One can clearly see, even with an 'average sized' mortgage, people in certain parts of the world are getting majorly ripped off on all sorts of levels. How can you have a great quality of life if that life is predestined to paying back over-inflated prices? To me, the answer is clear.

Say goodbye, move countries and be free of stress so you can claim back your life, time and energy.

Step-by-Step Guide to Buying Property in France

So you've finally found your dream home and now you're wondering what comes next?

Here's a brief guide:

- If you don't speak French hire a translator (so you know what's in the contracts).
- Make an offer (less than the listed price).
- Ask whether the listed price includes commission (usually 6-8 percent).
- Ask about the *notaire's* fees (about 6 percent).
- The agent is legally required to pass on the offer to the seller, even if they don't like it/ agree with it. Once you make the offer you've basically committed to the purchase.
- If the seller agrees to your offer, they need to send a letter stating they agree.
- After you receive the letter, you get 7 days to change your mind without being penalized.
- There's no need to pay a deposit when you make the offer (it's against the law for them to ask you to).You hand over a deposit when the sale (not the offer) is made.
- In France you need to use a *notaire* (a publicly appointed official) when purchasing property (not the agent). The *notaire* needs to make sure that you know exactly what you're signing. Legally, he/she is required to do so, hence don't be afraid to ask questions.
- Once you've signed the contract you are obligated to buy the property (subject to the 7-day 'cooling off' period and/or any other conditions).
- Before the contract closes, go and check the house to make sure everything is as it should be, i.e., that nothing is missing etc.

Warning! Unlike the States and Australia, the seller is not required to point out potential problems with the property, so you'll need to check things out yourself and/or take a building inspector with you. Take photos of potential problems, if necessary.

How to spot a good real estate agent

If you're dealing with a good agent, you should expect to receive a lot of help during the whole buying process. After all, you're the boss and you're entitled to as much help as you need. Here are a couple of things to look out for:

- How long have they been in business?
- Are they registered with the fnaim, http://www.fnaim.fr/, which is essentially a network/registry of all qualified agents?
- 4-10 percent of fees should be negotiable.
- Can they provide help with local knowledge (recommend a good doctor, dentist, bank)?
- Is there an after sales service or does the service end when you've handed over the hard cash?
- Are they prepared to drive you to different viewings?
- Do they have a good relationship with the local *notaire*?

Renovation Tips

- There are no surveys here because a lot of properties are ancient, but try to get a builder to take a closer look.
- Give yourself more time. Usually more than estimated because everything takes longer. Once again, you need patience.
- For exterior renovations you need permission from the local mairie. (You don't need permission for interior renovations).
- Hire an architect and get some decent drawings done (ask at the *mairie* as they're usually helpful in these areas).
- If you use a French builder ask him for a proper quote, which can be offset on capital gains tax if you sell at later stage.
- Talk to people, get advice, you're bound to find lots of English speaking people anyway (France is riddled with them).

French Real Estate, De-Mystified

I love surfing the net for international property. In fact it's one of my favorite things to do. Good thing is, I'm getting better at it. Don't know about you, but when I first started browsing the Internet for real estate bargains, I'd usually click on the first couple of sites I came across. Inevitably they'd be the most expensive, or else they were confusing and frustrating, sending me on a wild goose chase.

Back then, I often thought, if only I had a list of local agents without all the bells and whistles I could bypass all the money sharks and cut to the chase, which is precisely the reason I've included this chapter.

Normally when you read articles that contain a handful of 'recommended' real estate agents, chances are they've paid to advertise within the article. Not necessarily your best option.

Ultimately it's in my best interest to sell valuable information rather than advertising space, which is why the agencies list is made up of agents I've come across in my travels. None of which have paid me a dime. They are regional, as well as neighborhood agents I found via brochures and pamphlets.

For those who are seriously searching for the right property in France, the information in this section alone is all you will ever need.

Note:

I've included a lot of smaller type agents you would otherwise never find.

Also included are the locally popular 'classifieds' sites.

Likewise, some 'off the plan new development' sites for people who may be interested in purchasing a brand new, carefree beach condo.

Some sites are in English, some bilingual/multilingual and some in French. It's best to conduct the searches in French (even if you don't speak a word of it). Why? For example, if you were to type in 'Real estate for sale in Paris', you'd get all the International sites trying to sell you a piece of French paradise (via their UK or wherever else based business which means majorly inflated prices). If on the other hand you typed in '*Immobilier Paris*', you will find local agents with local prices. It's as simple as that.

As long as you become familiar with the search criteria terms you'll be fine (see 'real estate jargon' below).

Once you find a couple of places you like you can enquire further using simple sentences via **'google translate'**. Remember to keep it simple, because google doesn't do complicated sentences or subtext. When you write, ask if anybody in the office speaks English. If not, just 'google translate' their response from French to English.

With **'google maps'** you can literally see a street on the other side of the world. With 'satellite google maps' http://www.maps.google.com/- you can (in some cases) check out the front door of a house/apartment building in France from your lounge room in America.

You'll notice that the sizes of apartments and studios are a lot smaller than you're used to - a matter of adaptation (by now, you already know I'm a small house/apartment enthusiast). As far as I'm concerned, the smaller the better (within reason). Small means less tax, less cleaning, less to fix, less to worry about, less junk, less clutter. Lock up and go.

Ultimately, no matter how old my little ebook gets, the information on the websites will always be up to date on what's available (provided the businesses haven't closed for whatever reason).

Moving right along…

Conducting real estate searches in French can be a little confusing. If you don't know what to look for/ which words are which, here's a basic run down:

French Real Estate Jargon

Departement (department or area of France)

Vente (Sale)

Louer (Rent)

Prix min (Enter minimum price requirement)

Prix max (Enter maximum price requirement)

Surface min (Enter minimum surface area required)

Surface max (Enter maximum surface area required)

Pièces min (minimum number of rooms required)

Pièces max (maximum number of rooms required)

Code Postal (enter the post code of area you're interested in. Often this is optional but you can easily look them up in google)

Afficher les photos (means you're only interested in seeing properties with photos attached – highly recommended!)

Trier par prix (sort by price)

Viager occupe – if this category/offer looks too good to be true, that's because it is. Basically, these words mean you buy the heavily discounted property from an elderly person. You then pay them a monthly allowance until the day they die. Sometimes the buyer ends up dying before the original owner, and this happens all the time, which is why it's a risky business, so please tread carefully.

Maison (house)

Apartment (just what it says)

Terrain (land)

Parking (parking spot)

Autre (other)

Immobilier de Particulier A Particulier (private listings by owner), here's an example: http://www.entreparticuliers.com/

For a more detailed guide to French real estate listings/jargon, check out:

https://www.angloinfo.com/france/how-to/france-housing-property-jargon

France Regions and Real Estate Prices Overview

(Including detailed links to latest listings)

Before we plunge in and search for your dream home, consider the following:

I usually search for bargain properties hence, feel free to change the search criteria (price, size, apartment, house, land, etc according to your personal tastes/budget).

To get to the 'next page' click on *"page suivante"* (bottom left corner of each real estate page).

If some of the bargain properties look too good to be true, that's because they are. Don't go for anything that says *"Viager Occupe"* in the description (as aforementioned, this means you buy the property from an elderly person at a cheap price and pay them a monthly allowance until they die. Often the buyer dies before the original owner dies. Sad but true).

Ok, ready? Here's a breakdown and brief description of regions, including links to the latest bargain properties available.

Alsace

Half-timbered houses with overflowing geranium window boxes. Quaint picture book villages spread amongst vineyards; Alsace, in the north-east of France is the smallest of the French regions but huge in terms of cultural identity. A region loved for its enchanting architecture, mind-blowing landscapes, delicious local wines, beer and gastronomic delights.

Departments: Bas-Rhin and Haut-Rhin.

Check out the link below for chalets and character houses under €50 000…

http://www.leboncoin.fr/ventes_immobilieres/offres/alsace/?f=a&th=1&pe=2&ret=1

Aquitaine

World-renowned vineyards, delicious food, a rich heritage and a huge calendar of annual festivals (including Bullfighting). The Aquitaine region in the south-west, is one of France's largest. Popular with tourists and French people alike, who flock there annually to soak up the 200km stretch of gorgeous, white and sandy Atlantic coast.

Perfect for those who prefer a trendy/touristy, yet more laid back alternative to the packed Mediterranean. With a backdrop of pine forest, the Pyrenees mountain range and some of France's most celebrated villages and vineyards, what more could you ask for?

Departments: Dordogne, Gironde, Landes, Lot et Garonne, Pyrénées-Atlantiques

For apartments under €50 000.

http://www.leboncoin.fr/ventes_immobilieres/offres/aquitaine/?f=a&th=1&pe=2&ret=2

Auvergne

Probably the least known and most remote region is the largest, unspoiled and environmentally protected, (central) area in France. Here you can literally walk on extinct volcanoes and immerse yourself in dense forests, vast gorges, lakes, streams and rivers.

Auvergne is a nature lover's paradise attracting many people seeking relief from arthritis and various other ailments in mineral hot and cold-water springs. The area is famous for its hearty, rural cuisine and delicious blue cheese. Departments: Allier, Cantal, Haute Loire, Puy de Dome.

There's a mountain of real estate bargains to be had here. You can find entire deserted villages in the region. If the cold weather doesn't bother you, here's what €50 000 will buy you.

http://www.leboncoin.fr/ventes_immobilieres/offres/auvergne/?f=a&th=1&pe=2&ret=1

Burgundy

Peaceful Burgundy at the heart of France offers a rich history, gorgeous towns, villages and castles, plus 1200km of canals providing inland waterways for cruising on your newly acquired houseboat....

http://www.leboncoin.fr/nautisme/offres/auvergne/occasions/?f=a&th=1&q=Peniche

Perfect for walking, cycling and the like. Although this area is not the most popular with expats, it does attract its fair share of Parisians looking for weekend retreats (obviously they know where to bag a bargain).

If you love Paris, but can't afford it, this could be the perfect alternative because the area is only 100km south of Paris. It's here that you'll find loads of inexpensive village and farm houses, granges and barns in need of a bit of TLC. Cheap as chips, plenty of charm.

Here, gastronomes will track down some excellent meats, free-range poultry, truffles, snails, mouth-watering mushrooms and wine - lets not forget the wine people!

Departments: Cote d'Or, Nièvre, Saone et Loire, Yonne

Real estate bargains for under €50 000 see below:

http://www.leboncoin.fr/ventes_immobilieres/offres/bourgogne/?f=a&th=1&pe=2&ret=1

Brittany

Medieval villages, 1110 km of endless coasts, rugged cliffs, sandy beaches - perfect for swimming, sailing, wind surfing, and scuba-diving. Probably best to give the swimming part a miss during the wet, cold and windy winters. Apart from that, the climate is fairly mild (due to the Gulf Stream).

Brittany accounts for around 10 percent of France's agriculture (cauliflower and artichokes) and fishing productions. The area also produces cider, artisanal beers and whiskey (good for keeping warm).

Traditionally, the Britones like to drink plenty of cider to wash down their famous sweet crepes and salty galettes amongst other local staples – seafood, mussels, oysters, artichokes, potatoes, cabbage, salt and butter. Departments: Cotes d'Armor, Finistere, Ille et Vilaine, Morbihan.

Some Real Estate love here:

http://www.leboncoin.fr/ventes_immobilieres/offres/bretagne/?f=a&th=1&pe=2&ret=1

Center

The 'heart of France', also known as The Loire Valley, Central Loire or Val de Loire, boasts a rich, fertile land, medieval and renaissance architecture and a temperate climate. Because of that, the area is perfect for walking and cycling along the many rivers and lakes - and/or picnicking alongside endless fields of sunflowers. Apart from the wine, the Center's main agriculture revolves around beetroots, leeks, red onions, cucumbers and sunflowers.

Lovers of French country food known as "Cuisine du Terroir" flock here for the gourmet goats cheese (Sainte Maure), traditional French pork sausages cooked in wine and the locally famous Tarte Tatin (apple pie). Departments: Eure-et-Loir, Indre, Indre-et-Loire, Loir-et-Cher, Loiret.

Think this could be your perfect spot? See below for local bargains:

http://www.leboncoin.fr/ventes_immobilieres/offres/centre/?f=a&th=1&pe=2&ret=1

Champagne-Ardenne

North-east of France sits the region most of us know by name only. It offers plenty of parks, forests, and lakes - not to mention all those vineyards producing the bubbly responsible for making us do silly things.

Apart from its glamorous grapes used in the production of champagne, the region also grows far less glamorous crops such as maize, wheat, cabbage and sugar beet. Local gastronomy traditions and specialities include cheese, sausages, biscuits, cider and wine.

Until recently not overly popular with expats and overseas buyers, this part of France is nonetheless attracting more and more British buyers each year. And though prices have increased by around 70 percent in the past five years, the area still provides plenty of cheap farmhouses as well as traditional houses and apartments to renovate. Departments: Ardennes, Aube, Haute Marne, Marne.

Sneak a peek here:

http://www.leboncoin.fr/ventes_immobilieres/offres/champagne_ardenne/?f=a&th=1&pe=2&sqs=5&ret=1&ret=2

Corsica

The island of Corsica, situated some 160km off the southern coast of France boasts some of the finest powder sand and turquoise bay beaches in the Mediterranean, if not the world.

What's more, a no high-rise developments rule on the island allows for a total picture book ideal that doesn't stop at the spectacular beaches. The island's interior is a herb scented garden paradise, covered in steep mountains, rustic villages and rich olive grove valleys.

The Island's half-French, half-Italian mentality and culture is due to the fact that the French bought it (from the Republic of Genoa) in 1764. After a short civil war in 1768-69, it was incorporated into France in 1770. (Probably why Corsicans are reputed to be unapproachable and reserved when it comes to strangers).

Clearly, Corsica's relationship with France's mainland remains somewhat strained. Even so, plenty of

French people live and holiday on the island, a secret hot spot for French and European artists and celebrities alike.

The local cuisine is delicious and strictly seasonal. The meat is mostly free-range and because the animals get to graze on exquisite herbs and plants, it gives the meat a high quality and a very distinctive color and taste. Other local delights include, honey, fish, cheese and fruit.

As yet, Corsica is fairly unpopular with overseas investors. Reasons? Firstly there's the islands volatile history. Secondly, nobody knows about the place (world's best secret as far as yours truly is concerned). And thirdly, the property prices are relatively high when compared to the rest of France (albeit not the rest of the world). Departments: Corse du Sud, Haute Corse :

For properties under €100 000...
http://www.leboncoin.fr/ventes_immobilieres/offres/corse/?f=a&th=1&pe=4&ret=1&ret=2

Franche Comté

Located in the east of France (along the Vosges and Jura Mountains) sits a region that boasts timbered houses with breathtaking views, lush, rolling hills, thick pine forest, cleansing waterfalls, gorges and crystal lakes. This lesser known and relatively wild region of France shares much of its culture, cuisine and architecture with Switzerland, its neighbor.

French food gourmets will revel in the rustic local cuisine made by following centuries old traditions....famous smoked sausages like Saucisse de Morteau and Saucisse Montbéliard...the excellent variety of Franche Comté cheeses made from unpasteurized cow's milk...and wattle and fir tree honey that's been produced in the area since the 18th century.

For second (or permanent) homebuyers in quest of a traditional village or city life surrounded by nature, this could very well be your dream region :

http://www.leboncoin.fr/ventes_immobilieres/offres/franche_comte/?f=a&th=1&pe=2&ret=1

Departments: Doubs, Haute Saone, Jura, Territoire de Belfort

Languedoc Roussillon

This hugely popular area in the south-west of France ticks all the boxes. It's perfectly situated along the Mediterranean and the Pyrenees - bordering with Spain and Andorra in the south.

With plenty of sunshine, cheap real estate, hearty food, a diverse landscape and never ending stretches of coast...interspersed with a mix of lively cities, quaint fishing villages and stunning medieval architecture - it looks like hanging about in this beautiful region could add up to some pretty good living.

Locally produced gastronomic delights include: Olive oil, tomatoes, seafood and wine (with vineyards stretching over 300 000 hectares across the region). A version of the Cassoulet (there are many) - a French bean, sausage and pork sensation is a well-known Languedoc staple, along with traditional fish specialities like Bourride de Baudroie, Bourride Sètoise and Brandade de Morue (mashed cod with garlic, olive oil and a touch of cream topped with a layer of potato puree).

Local Real Estate Bargains:
http://www.leboncoin.fr/ventes_immobilieres/offres/languedoc_roussillon/?f=a&th=1&pe=2&sqs=5&ret=1&ret=2

Departments: Aude, Gard, Herault, Lozère, Pyrénées-Orientales

Limousin

The heartland of France is perfect for those looking for tranquility somewhere remote and rural in a picturesque setting dotted by charming villages amongst plenty of green, untapped woodland.

Into the bargain, the area is a water-sports lovers dream, with plenty of rivers, deep gorges and hundreds of lakes setting the perfect scene for sailing, fishing, canoeing and general splashing about.

If you're a nature lover, prepare to be seduced by this tiny region in central France, which is actually better known and loved by foreigners (in particular the British) than the French themselves.

Living costs and properties are cheaper than in some neighboring regions, which is why potential newcomers are beginning to catch on. If your heart is set on a charming renovation property in a typical village or town with plenty of character and a great way of life, then this could be the one:

http://www.leboncoin.fr/ventes_immobilieres/offres/limousin/?f=a&th=1&pe=2&sqs=5&ret=1

Departments: Correze, Creuse, Haute Vienne

Lorraine

Also know as the land of the three frontiers, (Pays de Trois Frontières), this far north-eastern part of France shares borders (and a complex political history) with Germany, Luxemburg and Belgium, It's rolling hills and rich soil support a mix of dairy farming, wheat and oats, meaning the landscape is heavily influenced by agricultural plains and industry, although it does boast some fantastic architecture.

Gastronomy drawing cards include the word famous Quiche Lorraine, almond Macarons, Bergamotes confectionery, Madeleines cookies and some pretty fine wines like the famous Gris de Toul (Grey wine from Toul), which is essentially a grey rosé.

Although well known by the British, the region is not the most popular choice for foreign second-home buyers (perhaps due to its rather bleak history), but it offers a typical easy going French lifestyle, cute villages and great towns (like Nancy) surrounded by an abundance of nature. What's more, properties are comparatively large and prices are low. See for yourself:

http://www.leboncoin.fr/ventes_immobilieres/offres/lorraine/?f=a&th=1&pe=2&sqs=5&ret=1&ret=2

Departments: Meurthe et Moselle, Meuse, Moselle, Vosges

Lower Normandy

Located in the north-western coast of France, Lower Normandy boasts popular seaside towns, a historic coastline, highly fertile land, rich pastures and densely wooded areas perfect for walking where you can spot plenty of wildlife such as deer and wild boar. Evidently, the area is popular with deer hunters and mushroom hunters alike. Just in case you didn't know, the French go crazy during mushroom season (November-December), although in Normandy you'll probably find them all year long.

Lower Normandy (Basse Normandie) is famous for producing butter, cheese (camembert), apple cider, and apple flavoured liquor. The area is an absolute heaven for meat lovers, wine lovers and foodies chasing some traditional French cooking. Departments: Calvados, Manche, Orne. For houses and apartments under €50 000 see below :

http://www.leboncoin.fr/ventes_immobilieres/offres/basse_normandie/?f=a&th=1&pe=2&ret=1&ret=2

Midi Pyrenees

Located in the south of France close to the Atlantic coastline, this - the largest region of France (equivalent in size to Switzerland and Luxemburg combined) offers extraordinary landscapes, mountain scenery, pine woods, sandy beaches and tiny thyme scented valleys covered in thick forest.

Location wise alone, the region is a star…the Atlantic, the Mediterranean, the Pyrenees and the gorgeous city of Toulouse with its many shops, and museum, all within easy reach. Evidently, in more ways than one, the ever popular, diverse and receptive to newcomers 'Midi', represents the ideal way of life for a multitude of foreign buyers.

Midi Gastronomy is a fine balance between French and Spanish cultures - rich in local gourmet delights and country cooking. Local specialties include mountain cheese, red peppers, rich tomatoes, Bayonne ham, truffles and walnut oil.

Departments: Ariège, Aveyron, Gers, Haute Garonne, Hautes-Pyrénées, Lot, Tarn, Tarn et Garonne

Take a look at some cheap properties in The Midi:

http://www.leboncoin.fr/ventes_immobilieres/offres/midi_pyrenees/?f=a&th=1&pe=2&ret=1&ret=2

Nord Pas de Calais

Bordering Belgium, the English Channel and the North Sea, the most northern part of France (near Luxemburg) offers unspoilt nature, long sandy beaches, museums, fortified towns, woodlands, fresh food markets, stunning villages, carnivals, friendly locals and good food.

Needless to say, due to the regions location and strong Flemish influence it's a popular spot for Belgian and British second homeowners alike.

Regional agriculture consists of potatoes, green beans, peas and chicory.

Top-notch gastronomic charms include the soft and creamy Maroilles cheese, beer and some lesser-known wines. Famous dishes include the classic Potjevleesch Meat Stew (made from chicken, rabbit and veal – served with chips and beer), local seafood, and the famous Betises de Cambrai minty sweets.

Some real estate steals:

http://www.leboncoin.fr/ventes_immobilieres/offres/nord_pas_de_calais/?f=a&th=1&pe=2&ret=1&ret=2

Departments: Nord, Pas de Calais

Paris Ile-de-France

Small in area, yet large in population, this region includes Paris and seven departments around the French capital, one of the most spectacular cities in the world. Without doubt, it's got everything a cosmopolitan city lover could possibly desire…museums, magnificent architecture, flea markets, parks, superb restaurants, the Seine, chic boutiques and more.

It's surrounding departments offering an abundance of lush greenery, lakes and forests, villages, not to mention plenty of cheap and charming properties… barns, cottages, chalets and maisons the village in quiet country settings to claim as your own.

Although it's the most expensive region in France it's still possible to find a studio in Paris for around €100 000 (though you won't find anything bigger than a broom cupboard). That being so, if you're in love with Paris, you really are better off living in one of the seven surrounding departments. It's what plenty of 'Parisians' do. That way you get more for you buck, a better lifestyle surrounded by nature and Paris at your feet.

For a mix of country homes and apartments in and near Paris priced under €100 000: http://www.leboncoin.fr/ventes_immobilieres/offres/ile_de_france/?f=a&th=1&pe=4&ret=1&ret=2

Departments: Paris, Essonne, Hauts de Seine, Seine et Marne, Seine Saint, Denis, Val de Marne, Val d'Oise, Yvelines

Pays de la Loire

Wild, rocky coast, sandy beaches, a jade colored sea, offshore islands…rich leafy countryside…crystal clear rivers and rich vineyards blend to create a homebuyers dream.

This diverse region in western France (also referred to as the Loire Valley, or Western Loire) resides largely in the Massif Armoricain (an ancient mountain range). Winters are cold, summers are warm, and property prices are inexpensive.

Regional food temptations include Cendre au Beurre Blanc (soft water fish with butter sauce)…Rillettes (a paté based on pork meat), the world famous Sel de Guérande, Port Salut (semi-soft cheese), Petit Beurre (butter) biscuits and Muscadet wine, (a dry white wine consumed with oysters and seafood).

Note: In case you left your heart in Paris, the TGV from the city of Nantes (the regions capital) to the city of lights takes 2 hours.

For a range of stunning give-away properties check out this link:

http://www.leboncoin.fr/ventes_immobilieres/offres/pays_de_la_loire/?f=a&th=1&pe=2&ret=1

Departments: Loire Atlantique, Maine et Loire, Mayenne, Sarthe, Vendee

Picardie

Renowned for its rich history and culture, the northern region of Picardie offers old fashioned towns, unspoilt coastlines, quiet resorts, sandy beaches, Compiégne and Chantilly forests, lush valleys and rich meadows.

Due to its close proximity to Paris, the area is another hot spot for Parisian second-home owners, Calais and the rest of northern France. Easily accessible and served by low-budget airlines like Ryanair, this region offers a quiet lifestyle and great value for money bargain properties (in fact, some of the lowest in France).

Food and drink native to Picardie include the delicious Chantilly cream, leek tart, Gateau Battu (similar to Brioche), saucisson (dried sausage), duck, patés, terrines, wine, champagne, ciders and beers. For cheap property see below:

http://www.leboncoin.fr/ventes_immobilieres/offres/picardie/?f=a&th=1&pe=2&ret=1&ret=2

Departments: Aisne, Oise, Somme

Poitou Charentes

The district of Poitou Charentes sits about half way down the west coast. This largely unspoilt region along the Atlantic will appeal to lovers of architecture who appreciate historical monuments, coastal fortifications and ancient Roman constructions. The region is renowned for its seaside resorts, endless stretches of beach, a sunflower fields interior…thriving vineyards, lively outdoor markets…wild mushrooms galore…and marshes known as Marais Poitevin, which are Frances version of Venice.

Culinary treasures include, goat cheeses, Echiré butter, a paté (used for stuffing) called Farci Poitevin, Tourteau Fromagé (cheesecake), as well as meat, fish, and the locally produced, world-renowned Cognac.

The area is perfect for first or second-home buyers looking for a quiet lifestyle in a typical character-village setting with a well-preserved culture.

For homes under €50 000:

http://www.leboncoin.fr/ventes_immobilieres/offres/poitou_charentes/?f=a&th=1&pe=2&ret=1

Departments: Vienne, Deux Sevres, Charente, Charente Maritime

Provence Alpes Cote d'Azur

It's not difficult to see why people flock here in droves. The fabulous French Riviera - probably the most famous and sought-after region in the south-east of France is also the most expensive (with a couple of exceptions).

The light, color and atmosphere - a dream setting and inspiration for many artist including Paul Cézanne and Matisse…the coastline and lovely beaches of the Mediterranean Sea…lavender scented Provence…its ideal position between Italy and Spain. The rich history, culture…gorgeous properties, impressive villas, castles, and medieval villages perched on mountain tops are only some of the charms the south has on offer.

Famous culinary treats include Nicoise Salad, Ratatouille, Bouillabaisse (fish stew), seafood, Tapenade, Pistou, adorned with plenty of local olive oil, garlic, spices, and herbes de Provence (wash it down, with a great deal of fresh and fruity Cotes de Provence Rosé).

Although comparatively expensive, there are still plenty of bargain properties around. If you like cities, check out Marseille. If you're after something a little more rural, the Var offers an abundance of character village houses, apartments, ruins and barns to restore.

For houses under €100 000, search here:

http://www.leboncoin.fr/ventes_immobilieres/offres/provence_alpes_cote_d_azur/?f=a&th=1&pe=4&ret=1

For studios, apartments and time-share (Multi propriété) properties under €50 000:

http://www.leboncoin.fr/ventes_immobilieres/offres/provence_alpes_cote_d_azur/?f=a&th=1&pe=2&ret=2

For land under €50 000 (some with tiny chalets, and re-constructible ruins):

http://www.leboncoin.fr/ventes_immobilieres/offres/provence_alpes_cote_d_azur/?f=a&th=1&pe=2&ret=3

Departments: Alpes de Haute Provence, Hautes Alpes, Alpes Maritimes, Bouches du Rhone, Var, Vaucluse

Rhone Alps

Bordering Italy and Switzerland just north of Provence-Alpes-Cote-d'Azur lies some of the most spectacular landscape in France. Snow capped peaks, (including Mont Blanc, the highest mountain in Europe at 15 771 feet)...hundreds of kilometers of ski-slopes...glaciers...a bounty of national parks...story book villages, some of the finest vineyards.

One can imagine hiking through carpets of wild mountain flowers, aromatic lavender fields, swimming in fresh, crystal clear lakes. This region is a contrast of busy ski resorts, remote rural life and well-kept traditions.

Note: It needs to be said that there is in fact some heavy industry (including 5 nuclear power stations) along the banks of the Rhone River. That being so, it doesn't seem to bother people all that much. Not the locals. Not the investors. If it doesn't bother you *non plus*, go ahead and check out this link for houses under €50 000.

http://www.leboncoin.fr/ventes_immobilieres/offres/rhone_alpes/?f=a&th=1&pe=2&ret=1

For similarly priced apartments and studios:

http://www.leboncoin.fr/ventes_immobilieres/offres/rhone_alpes/?f=a&th=1&pe=2&ret=2

Departments: Ain, Ardèche, Drome, Haute-Savoie, Isère, Loire, Rhone, Savoie

Upper Normandie

Pebble beaches, milky-white cliffs, unexpected rock formations and tiny villages strewn along the coast...Haute Normandie, in the northwest hosts a couple of the biggest ports in France (Le Havre and Dieppe). And just as well. Visitors from the UK, flock there in droves to catch one of the best street markets in northern France and sample seafood straight off the boats.

Naturally, due to the close proximity to the UK, the spectacular scenery and shared historic past, this dynamic region is an extremely sought after destination amongst the British.

The inland is reminiscent of a landscape painting…with cattle grazing on rich pastures…plentiful orchards…countless streams…rustic, wood framed houses alongside modern buildings.

Regional gourmet delights include fresh seafood, oysters, scallops and dishes like Hareng Saur (Smoked Herring), Marmite Dieppoise (Fish Stew), Omeletes, Neufchatel cheese, apple pie, cider and Calvados.

Due to the areas popularity, real estate prices are slightly higher but if you want a place to renovate you can still find some half-timbered houses, farmhouses and cottages at a reasonable price. Here's what on offer for under €100 000:

http://www.leboncoin.fr/ventes_immobilieres/offres/haute_normandie/?f=a&th=1&pe=4&ret=1

Departments: Eure, Seine Maritime

List of Real Estate Agents

If you're unsure where or how to start looking for your dream home, this list will give you the edge on around 99 percent of people. Click on the links and be transported to your dream home…

Nice, Cannes & Surrounding Regions

http://www.agence-centrale-laciotat.com

http://www.agence-contesso.com

http://www.agence-ecid.com

http://www.agence-hippodrome.com

http://www.agencedesarts.fr

http://www.agencelacanopee.com

http://www.agencelaurentine.com

http://www.agencemercure-cannes.com

http://www.akorimmo.com

http://www.antibes-sud-immobilier.com

http://www.avpimmo.com

http://www.barsurloup-immo.com

http://www.bourgeois-immo.com

http://www.cabinetvogue.com

http://www.capsud-immobilier.com

http://www.citya.com

http://www.climmo.com

http://www.cogimmo.com

http://www.conseilsgestion.fr

http://www.crouzet-breil.com

http://www.damonte-immobilier.com

http://www.dgimmo.fr

http://www.easy-immobilier.com

http://www.easyhomeriviera.com

http://www.etoileimmo.com

http://www.fusini-immobilier.com

http://www.gecko-immobilier.com

http://www.griguer-immobilier.com

http://www.groupegambetta.fr

http://www.ifc06.com

http://www.immo-terrasse.com

http://www.velmerimmobilier.com

http://www.laforet.com/agence-immobiliere/nice-centre

http://www.immobiliereroseland.fr

http://www.immoprojet.fr

http://www.immotende.com

http://www.inter-immo06.com

http://www.interimmobilier-nice.fr

http://www.italgestgroup.com

http://www.lorana-properties.com

http://www.maisonsbeatrice.com

http://www.martine-schellino.com

http://www.michelyneastier.fr

http://www.nexity-logement.com

http://www.nice-properties.fr

http://www.orpi.com
http://www.petitjuasimmobilier.com
http://www.portimmo.com
http://www.prestigimmo.fr
http://www.promogim.fr
http://www.renoir-immobilier.com

http://www.revellimmo.fr
http://www.ladresse-saintlaurentduvar.com/
http://www.votre-agence-immo.fr

Marseille, Aubagne, Aix-En Provence Regions
http://www.adeptimmo.fr
http://www.ahoraimmobilier.com
http://www.buech-devoluy.com
http://www.cabinet-canovas.com
http://www.carnoux-immobilier.com
http://www.century21.fr
http://www.espaces-atypiques.com/marseille/
http://www.cornicheimmo.com
http://www.foncia.com
http://www.ibh-immobilier.com
http://www.immobagne.com
http://www.immobilier-recouly.com
http://www.immodefrance.com
http://www.ladressemarseille.com
http://www.laforet-immobilier-marseille-7eme.com
http://www.lamy.net
http://www.limmobiliersurmesure.fr
http://www.marseille-immodupalais.fr
http://www.otimimmobilier.com
http://www.quorum-immobilier.com

http://www.rond-point-immobilier.com

http://www.immo-delatour.com

http://www.immo-victoria.com

http://www.laure-immobilier-marseille.com

http://www.perimmo.fr

http://www.marseillaisedimmobilier.com

http://www.micheldechabannes.fr

http://www.immobiliere-lemarquis.fr

http://www.immobiliere-lieutaud.com

http://www.quorum-immobilier.com

http://www.topimmobiliermarseille.com

http://www.ericsimon-immobilier.fr

http://www.immocube.fr

Other Regions

http://www.francesud.fr (Var region)

http://www.grechimmo.com (Bandol, Brignoles, Hyères, Toulon etc)

http://www.immobilier-forcalquier.com- (Provence)

http://www.twimmo.com/ (Rhone Alpes)

http://www.immobilier-petits-prix.com (central France, low prices)

http://www.immobilieralsace.fr (lists several agencies Alsace Region)

http://www.immosaintevictoire.com (Aix en Provence and surrounds)

http://www.immosoleil.fr (La Ciotat)

http://www.immoventedirect.com (private sales, no commission, all over France)

http://www.laprovence-immo.com (Provence)

http://www.pasdagence.com - (privates for sale and rent, no commission)

http://www.passemard-immobilier.com (Midi-Pyrénéés)

http://www.saintpierreimmobilier.fr (Nice, Vence, Roquefort Les Pins etc)

http://www.secic.fr (Corse/Corsica)

http://www.solvimo.com (National)

http://www.sovagim.com (Les Arcs, Draguignan, Salernes, Le Muy etc)

http://www.st-jeannet-immo.com (St Jeannet)

http://www.transaxia.fr (specializing in areas in the center of France)

http://www.valerie-immobilier-peillot.com (St Laurent to Var)

http://www.agencearnaud.com (St Cyr Sur Mer, Le Castellet, etc)

http://www.explorimmo.com/ (National)

http://www.site-pap.fr/site-immobilier-paris-75-g439 (Private sales, National)

Classified Listings

http://www.leboncoin.fr/

(National Classifieds, choose the area, then choose 'ventes immobilieres' in drop-down menu)

http://www.paruvendu.fr/ (National Classifieds)

http://www.entreparticuliers.com/ (National private sales)

http://www.pap.fr/annonce/vente-immobiliere (National private sales)

Secret Real-Estate Hot Spots

Creuse in the Limousin region of France is one of the least visited places by foreigners because there's not a lot of 'touristy' stuff to do and see. But it does have the type of unspoilt landscape reminiscent of France in the 1950's. Plenty of rivers and lakes surrounded by green hills, valleys, forests and wildlife – not to mention welcoming and helpful locals.

Here's what's available for under €50 000:

http://www.leboncoin.fr/ventes_immobilieres/offres/limousin/?f=a&th=1&pe=2&ret=1&q=Creuse

The picture postcard village of **Ahetze** in the Basque province of Labourd is only 20 minutes from Biarritz. Surrounded by endless forests, stunning views, there are plenty of cute villages and divine beaches to explore all within a short radius. There's a huge flea market every third Sunday of the month. Unfortunately you won't find too many bargain properties, but to give you an idea, here's what you will find:

http://www.leboncoin.fr/ventes_immobilieres/offres/aquitaine/?f=a&th=1&ret=1&ret=2&q=Ahetze

Tucked between Avignon and Arles in Provence are **Les Petit Alpilles,** (little Alpes) - a beautiful mountain range with plenty of olive groves, vineyards, blue sky and magic light surrounding its numerous tiny villages in the area. Here's what's available in Avignon and Arles for under €100 000

Avignon:

http://www.leboncoin.fr/ventes_immobilieres/offres/provence_alpes_cote_d_azur/?f=a&th=1&pe=4&ret=1&ret=2&q=Avignon

Arles:

http://www.leboncoin.fr/ventes_immobilieres/offres/provence_alpes_cote_d_azur/?f=a&th=1&pe=4&ret=1&ret=2&q=Arles

Velleron: is a small town (3077 inhabitants) situated between Cavaillon and Carpentras in Vaucluse. Walk along the banks of La Sorgue, visit the extraordinary farmers market, go fishing, explore ancient castles and soak up the atmosphere and traditions of a village life environment.

http://www.leboncoin.fr/ventes_immobilieres/offres/provence_alpes_cote_d_azur/?ret=1&ret=2&q=Velleron&sp=1

Want more? (check out the following)

The village of **Bouilland** in Burgundy

The **Canal du Midi** in Southern France

The city of **Lyon** (great indoor markets with high quality local produce)

The Pyrenees (excellent for cycling along the Tourmalet and meditation/walking retreats)

Mont Ventoux, east of Avignon

A little village called **Montner** (west of Perpignan)

The Hautes-Alpes selected as one of the best places to live (especially great for people 50+)

Correze, a department in south central France

Aveyron, a sparsely populated secret even the French don't know about

The quiet and green surroundings of the **Pyrénées-Atlantiques**

The ideally situated **Tarn** – in the Midi-Pyrénéés

Vendéé, this sunny corner in western France is a department in the Pays-d-la-loire

Vienne a character town south of Lyon (on the Rhone River)

The Gers – in the Midi Pyrénéés

Deux-Sèvres – in the west

Haute-Garonne – based on the quality of education, shopping and employment, this area in the southwest of France was voted the overall best for younger age groups and families.

Finding short (and long-term) rentals

Whether or not you're buying your own slice of paradise, you may need to find some temporary accommodation until you do. There are many options to choose from. You could rent a short-term apartment or house for a few weeks or months. Short-term rentals are generally more expensive because the places are fully furnished, but you can always negotiate. Same goes for long-term rentals (a year or more).

The best way to find places is by word of mouth or advertisements such as the daily newspapers or private advertisements known as "De particulier à particulier" (directly from the owners) website: http://www.pap.fr

If you have no idea where you want to be, as in which suburb etc, your best option is short-term rental (in a central location) until you do. Renting an apartment via the Internet, however, may be a tad risqué due to the fact that you haven't seen it. Photos can be deceiving, never mind the street, area, these are all things to consider.

For short-term rental

Try the French version of the 'yellow pages':

http://www.pagesjaunes.fr

and/or the sites listed below:

http://www.tourisme.fr

http://www.explorimmo.fr

http://www.avendrealouer.fr

http://www.seloger.fr

http://www.fnaim.fr

Remember, **louer** means rent, **acheter** to buy and **vente** means sale. Most of the websites these days have a translation option for English. They are not always perfect so (again, when in doubt use 'google translate') for particular terms you're not sure of. Again, if your French is zero, your best bet is to contact some real estate agents http://www.fnaim.fr, write them a brief note in English stating your requirements and see if any of them get back to you.

The foreign buyers market is huge in France; so I'd be surprised if there's not at least one person in the office brave enough to take you on. Remember the French may come across as confident but they're just as shy about speaking English as you are about speaking French.

Short and Long Term Rentals in Marseille

http://www.marseille-apartments.com/sl-marseille-short-term-rentals.html

http://www.locamarseille.com/

http://www.vrbo.com (vacation rentals by owners)

http://www.marseille.vivastreet.fr/annonces-location-appartement+marseille (private rentals, long term)

http://www.marseille.vivastreet.fr/annonces-location-vacances+marseille- classifieds (private vacation rentals) http://www.pap.fr/annonce/location-particulier-marseille-13-g12024-5 (private rentals and sales)

http://www.agencedestanneurs.com (long term rentals in Marseille)

Vacation Rentals in Paris

http://www.parisattitude.com/search2.asp

http://www.apartment-in-france.com/paris.htm

https://www.airbnb.com/s/Paris--France?page=1&s_tag=RUiy9rJA&allow_override%5B%5D=

Real Estate Extra - Buying Land

Although there's a lot of cheap and wonderful land available, most of it is useless because one is not allowed to build. Therefore, you'll need to search for land that doesn't state 'Terrain non constuctible'. You'll want to read 'Terrain constructible', and you'll find it, though prices are fairly steep.

Good thing is, you are permitted to renovate any existing ruin on the land (within the confines of its original size), as long as the ruin is legally registered. If one was a handy person one could literally pick something like this up for under $30 000 euro; I've seen them for as low as $22 000. Here's what I mean:

http://www.leboncoin.fr/ventes_immobilieres/offres/languedoc_roussillon/?f=a&th=1&pe=2&ret=1&ret=3&q=ruine

Epilogue

Many moons ago I saw Meryl Streep in a TV interview. Meryl is, and always will be one of my acting heroes. Needless to say, when asked what was important to her, I hung onto every word she said. Wanna know what she said?

"There must be food, there must be love and there must be wine".

Obviously Meryl's been to France at some stage in her life but that's beside the point. By now, she's probably forgotten she ever uttered the above, but I haven't because at the time, her words resonated (just as Basil's words resonated, at the beginning of this tale). Naturally, this begs the question…

What does one do when something resonates in one's heart and soul?

One learns to listen, just as one learns to crawl, walk, run and dance. Eventually, through listening, one learns to fly - preferably in the right direction.

If the basis of life is freedom then surely the meaning of life, purpose and reason for being here is to experience joy, new things, new opportunities and new feelings.

But isn't it also about the thrill of being alive, to feel life pouring through you? That being so, why not allow yourself to fall in love a little? Be seduced.

The greatest gift you can give yourself is to say YES to who you really are. And to do whatever it takes to live the life you dream of. If that means living your life in France then nothing and nobody can stop you. Nobody but you.

"Unless you move, the place where you are is the place where you will always be"

(Ashley Brilliant)

###

Thank you for taking the time to read my book. I hope you enjoyed reading it as much as I've enjoyed creating it. It is my deepest wish that the words contained within these pages nudged you a little closer to fulfilling your dream.

Love and Light Refreshments.

Tanja

XO

About the author

I write, read, roam. I learn, unlearn, relearn. My dreams are to live softly. To remain maladjusted. To continue to breathe outside the system and to explore the entire planet before it disappears. Freedom is my favorite topic. Inspiring, motivating and showing people how to live free is my passion.

Other books by Tanja Bulatovic:

French Men on Love & Women - https://www.amazon.com/dp/B01M184PUI

Connect with Me Online

Twitter: https://twitter.com/tanjabulatovic

Website: http://www.tanjabulatovic.com/

Facebook: https://www.facebook.com/FrenchMenOnLoveAndWomen/

Printed in Great Britain
by Amazon